T0316568

Cambridge Elements ≡

Elements in Child Development
edited by
Marc H. Bornstein
National Institute of Child Health and Human Development, Bethesda
Institute for Fiscal Studies, London
UNICEF, New York City

BILINGUAL DEVELOPMENT IN CHILDHOOD

Annick De Houwer
Harmonious Bilingualism Network
and University of Erfurt

CAMBRIDGE
UNIVERSITY PRESS

CAMBRIDGE
UNIVERSITY PRESS

University Printing House, Cambridge CB2 8BS, United Kingdom

One Liberty Plaza, 20th Floor, New York, NY 10006, USA

477 Williamstown Road, Port Melbourne, VIC 3207, Australia

314–321, 3rd Floor, Plot 3, Splendor Forum, Jasola District Centre, New Delhi – 110025, India

79 Anson Road, #06–04/06, Singapore 079906

Cambridge University Press is part of the University of Cambridge.

It furthers the University's mission by disseminating knowledge in the pursuit of education, learning, and research at the highest international levels of excellence.

www.cambridge.org
Information on this title: www.cambridge.org/9781108791397
doi: 10.1017/9781108866002

First published 2021

A catalogue record for this publication is available from the British Library.

ISBN 978-1-108-79139-7 Paperback
ISSN 2632-9948 (online)
ISSN 2632-993X (print)

Bilingual Development in Childhood

Elements in Child Development

DOI: 10.1017/9781108866002
First published online: April 2021

Annick De Houwer
Harmonious Bilingualism Network and University of Erfurt

Author for correspondence: Annick De Houwer, annick.dehouwer@habilnet.org

Abstract: In the first decade of life, children become bilingual in different language learning environments. Many children start learning two languages from birth (Bilingual First Language Acquisition). In early childhood hitherto monolingual children start hearing a second language through day care or preschool (Early Second Language Acquisition). Yet other hitherto monolingual children in middle childhood may acquire a second language only after entering school (Second Language Acquisition). This Element explains how these different language learning settings dynamically affect bilingual children's language learning trajectories. All children eventually learn to speak the societal language, but they often do not learn to fluently speak their non-societal language and may even stop speaking it. Children's and families' harmonious bilingualism is threatened if bilingual children do not develop high proficiency in both languages. Educational institutions and parental conversational practices play a pivotal role in supporting harmonious bilingual development.

Keywords: bilingual, children, learning, language, acquisition

ISBNs: 9781108791397 (PB), 9781108866002 (OC)
ISSNs: 2632-9948 (online), 2632-993X (print)

Contents

1 Introduction

This Element concerns young children growing up with more than a single spoken language. Three life stages form its organizing structure (Steinberg et al., 2011, p. 5): (i) infancy, until about age 2 (infants); (ii) early childhood, until about age 6 (toddlers and preschoolers); and (iii) middle childhood, to about age 11 (schoolchildren).

The transitions between (i) and (ii) and between (ii) and (iii) coincide with fundamental changes in children's language use worldwide. When infants begin to speak, they do so mostly in just single words. Shortly before their second birthdays, toddlers combine words into short units that start to resemble sentences. Around age 6, schoolchildren start to learn to read and write.

Many newborns start hearing two languages from birth. This is a Bilingual First Language Acquisition (BFLA) language learning setting (Meisel, 1989). BFLA children have no experience with monolingualism. They are learning Language A and Language Alpha (Wölck, 1987/1988). This terminology expresses the lack of chronological difference between languages in terms of first regular exposure.

Other children first hear just a single language. For many of these initially monolingually reared children the transition between stages (i) and (ii) coincides with fundamental changes in linguistic environment: Children may start to regularly hear a second language through day care or preschool. Children who grew up monolingually in a first language (L1) but start regularly hearing a second language (L2) in late infancy or early childhood are growing up in an Early Second Language Acquisition (ESLA) setting (De Houwer, 1990).

For yet other initially monolingually reared children, it is the transition between (ii) and (iii) that coincides with fundamental changes in linguistic environment. Children who grew up monolingually throughout infancy and early childhood may start attending school in a new second language (L2) that differs from the one people were talking to them before (their L1). These children in middle childhood are growing up in a Second Language Acquisition (SLA) setting (De Houwer, 2019c). The latter differs from ESLA because SLA schoolchildren are simultaneously learning not only to understand and speak but also to read and write the new L2.

Bilingual children in very early infancy are typically BFLA children. Bilingual children in late infancy and early childhood are either BFLA or ESLA children. Bilingual children in middle childhood include BFLA, ESLA, and SLA children (see Figure 1).

Figure 1 Three kinds of bilingual learning settings in three life stages
Legend: BFLA = Bilingual First Language Acquisition; ESLA = Early Second Language
Acquisition; SLA = Second Language Acquisition

Many people are bilingual because of a migration background. Bilingualism also occurs in regions where two or more languages have been used side by side for centuries, as in Papua New Guinea, much of South America, the Indian subcontinent, and many regions in North America and Europe (Bhatia & Ritchie, 2013). There is usually a social hierarchy between languages, with one particular language and its users having higher status, social value, and power. The language locally used in public life, government, and education tends to be the one with the most prestige and is henceforth called the societal language (Soc-L). All other languages are non-societal languages (Non-Soc-Ls). Non-Soc-Ls are not used in education (except in foreign language classes); what is a Non-Soc-L in one region may be a Soc-L in another. In some regions two languages may be used in public life or in schools, or the local Soc-L differs from that in other parts of the country, but even in those settings there is a language hierarchy. The specific language environments and local language hierarchies individuals find themselves in strongly influence their bilingualism (De Houwer & Ortega, 2019). Local language hierarchies likewise affect bilingual children, regardless of whether the bilingual environment is one of BFLA, ESLA, or SLA.

BFLA children may hear a Non-Soc-L and the Soc-L at home, or they may hear two Non-Soc-Ls at home and learn the Soc-L in an (E)SLA setting at (pre) school. Because we know hardly anything about BFLA children in the latter case, the review in this Element only considers BFLA children with a Non-Soc-L and the Soc-L at home. Families who speak a Non-Soc-L and the Soc-L with BFLA children usually want their children to learn to understand and speak both languages from the start (De Houwer, 2017c). There are emotional and cultural bonds with both languages, and children are typically expected to speak both at home. This is different for families with (E)SLA children, who only use a Non-Soc-L at home. These families generally have a much stronger emotional and cultural connection to the Non-Soc-L than to the Soc-L that children learn through day care or (pre)school: Children are expected to speak the Non-Soc-L at home, not the Soc-L.

The term "bilingual children" refers to typically developing, normally hearing children under age 12 who need to learn to communicate in more than a single language in daily life, leaving unspecified to what extent children are able to communicate in two languages. The focus is on the untutored, so-called "naturalistic" learning of several languages as a result of life circumstances that are not easy to change. Children are born into a bilingual family (BFLA). Children born into families speaking just a Non-Soc-L (ESLA and SLA) usually have no other choice than to attend (pre)school in a Soc-L that differs from the home language, and must learn to function in the Soc-L.

Aside from a Non-Soc-L and a Soc-L, children may learn a foreign language (For-L), that is, a language that is not a local Soc-L. The For-L may be a Non-Soc-L for some children in the classroom and a Soc-L in other regions and countries. Although a For-L often carries high prestige and its learning is an asset, learning a For-L well is not fundamental for children's future in a particular region: They do not need a For-L in daily life. In contrast, all children, bilingual and monolingual, need to learn the local Soc-L well to function in society. Furthermore, people's emotional and cultural connections with For-Ls are generally different from those they have with languages learned at home and/or through residence in a new country. Muñoz and Spada (2019) and Juan-Garau and Lyster (2019) offer overviews of For-L teaching and learning.

Much of the heavy social and financial investment in the early teaching of For-Ls (especially English) in Europe and elsewhere rests on the assumption that children need to learn a language from an early age to learn it well (De Houwer, 2015a). As summarized in Section 6, the joint findings from studies on child bilingual development in naturalistic settings do not support this notion of "the earlier, the better."

The focus in this Element is on oral language use (Tang & Sze, 2019, discuss how children acquire a spoken and a sign language or two sign languages; Murphy, 2018, reviews how bilingual children learn to read and write). Excluded from discussion are transnational adoptees who have replaced their L1 with a single L2 (Genesee & Delcenserie, 2016) and children with developmental challenges such as autism and Developmental Language Disorder (Marinis et al., 2017; Patterson & Rodríguez, 2016).

It is possible for children to hear more than two languages. In referring to bilingualism, this Element includes those more complex multilingual situations, although the research basis for early multilingual rather than narrowly bilingual development is still thin (some excellent studies are Chevalier, 2015; Cruz-Ferreira, 2006; Montanari, 2010). Children may acquire different varieties of the same language (e.g., Appalachian dialect and Standard

American English) or varieties of different languages (e.g., Mexican Spanish and Standard American English). Given the paucity of research on the first case (Chevrot & Ghimenton, 2019; Durrant et al., 2014), this Element exclusively refers to learning different languages, although learning very different varieties of what is considered the same language is also a form of bilingualism.

Child bilingualism is a widespread global phenomenon. Precise statistics are not available. The fact that many societies in the Global South[1] are highly multilingual (Bhatia & Ritchie, 2013) means that children living there come into contact with several languages as a normal part of everyday life. If children do not encounter several languages before starting school, they often learn an ex-colonial language at school that they do not hear at home but that functions as a Soc-L (e.g., French in the south of Morocco; English in South Africa). Children in the Global North[2] are more likely to live in societies dominated by a single language in which monolingual ideologies reign (Fuller, 2019). In many of those societies, various types of statistics suggest that a fifth to over a third of children do not solely hear a Soc-L at home: for instance, the 2016 Australian census[3] found that more than one fifth of people spoke another language than English at home; in Germany, well over a third of children under age 10 had a migration background in 2016 (Autorengruppe Bildungsberichterstattung, 2018) and thus may have heard another language than German at home; the United-States-based Annie E. Casey Foundation brought together data suggesting that 23% of US children speak a language other than English at home;[4] and survey data collected in the officially Dutch-speaking region of Flanders, Belgium, in the 1990s (De Houwer, 2003) suggested that in one out of eight families, children heard a language other than Dutch at home.

In what circumstances do children become bilingual? We know little about the proportions of BFLA, ESLA, and SLA children. However, BFLA may occur about three times as often as ESLA and SLA combined (calculation based on survey data from different continents in De Houwer, 2007 [$N = 1,899$; Belgium], and in Winsler et al., 2014a [$N = 1,900$; United States];

---

[1] North–South Divide in the World. (n.d.). *Wikipedia* [website]. https://en.wikipedia.org/wiki/North%E2%80%93South_divide_in_the_World

[2] North–South Divide in the World. (n.d.). *Wikipedia* [website]. https://en.wikipedia.org/wiki/North%E2%80%93South_divide_in_the_World.

[3] 2016 Census: Multicultural. (n.d.). Australian Bureau of Statistics [website]. abs.gov.au/ausstats/abs@.nsf/lookup/media%20release3

[4] Children Who Speak a Language Other than English at Home in the United States. (2020, October). The Annie E. Casey Foundation: Kids Data Center [website]. https://datacenter.kids count.org/

when families reported using two languages at home, children likely heard these from birth; when families used only a Non-Soc-L at home, children likely grew up with that language as an L1 and learned an L2 later). A rare study of 681 bilingual students in Germany probing children's language learning histories found that 51% of children had grown up in a BFLA setting, 24% in an ESLA setting, and 25% in an SLA setting (calculations based on several tables in Ahrenholz et al., 2013). A majority of bilingual children thus likely grow up bilingually from birth rather than with a single L1 that is later complemented by an L2.

Different language learning environments (BFLA, ESLA, and SLA) have different effects on bilingual children's language learning trajectories in the first decade of life. It is the main aim of this Element to elucidate these language learning trajectories. The online presentations HaBilNet Class 1: Trajectories for Early Bilingualism[5] and HaBilNet Class 2: BFLA Compared to ESLA[6] on the HaBilNet Vimeo channel offer a quick overview for BFLA and ESLA.

Lay people and researchers alike often want to know how bilingual children compare to monolingual peers in the single Soc-L monolinguals are learning. "Success" for bilinguals is frequently measured *solely* in terms of bilinguals' performance in the Soc-L compared to monolinguals. If bilinguals perform worse than monolinguals the blame is often laid with the fact that bilinguals are acquiring another language. Even though bilingual–monolingual comparisons can elucidate theoretical questions, a *unique* focus on how bilinguals resemble monolinguals in Soc-L performance rarely leads to a better understanding of child bilingualism. Bilingualism is not a sort of double monolingualism (Grosjean, 1989). This Element mainly discusses bilingual development on its own merit.

The review here is based on a wide array of data collection methods, ranging from detailed case studies based on parental diaries to parental surveys yielding information on thousands of children. Aside from parent reports, studies may rely on experiments, standardized language tests, specially designed tasks, or direct observations of children's language use. Studies report on individual children's language use or, as has been much more often the case of late, on levels of language use or language behavior that are averaged across groups of children (i.e., group studies).

Terms in this Element that are ambivalent as to whether they refer to ethnicity, citizenship, or language refer to language unless otherwise indicated. The

---

[5] HaBilNet [Screen name]. (2020, May 6). HaBilNet Class 1: Trajectories for Early Bilingualism [Video]. Vimeo. https://vimeo.com/415653440

[6] HaBilNet [Screen name]. (2020, May 9). HaBilNet Class 2: BFLA Compared to ESLA [Video]. Vimeo. https://vimeo.com/416621250

term "family" designates any private household made up of at least one child under age 12 and one adult who is responsible for the child. The term "parents" refers to the adult(s) who is/are part of such a family. This Element follows Bornstein's transactional and dynamic perspective on the family, according to which "[c]hild and parent bring distinctive characteristics to, and each changes as a result of, every interaction; both then enter the next round of interaction as changed individuals" (Bornstein, 2019, p. 279). At the same time, macrosystem patterns of beliefs and values influence the interpersonal experiences individuals have (Bornstein, 2009). The influence of such macrosystem patterns is particularly relevant to bilingual children and their families. Societal attitudes toward early bilingualism and the languages involved affect stances and behaviors toward bilingual children and their families and may affect their socioemotional well-being (De Houwer, 2020a). Educational approaches in (pre-) schools play a large role in this dynamic.

In addition to describing bilingual children's oral language learning trajectories, this Element examines the nature of children's bilingual language learning environments. Aside from aspects such as the quantity of child-directed speech, these environments include parental conversational practices and effects of the aforementioned language-related attitudes. A separate section (Section 5) briefly examines the possible role of socioeconomic status in bilingual development.

Children's language learning environments determine the degree to which they and their families experience harmonious bilingualism; that is, "a subjectively neutral or positive experience that members of a family in a bilingual setting have with aspects of that setting" (De Houwer, 2020a, p. 63). This Element concludes with a summary of the main points and a plea for more research attention to harmonious bilingualism.

In brief, this Element focuses on the oral language development of three kinds of bilingual children: (i) BFLA children acquiring a Non-Soc-L (Language A) and a Soc-L (Language Alpha) from birth (followed from infancy to middle childhood); (ii) ESLA children acquiring a Non-Soc-L as their L1 and a Soc-L as their L2 (traced from early to middle childhood); and (iii) SLA children acquiring a Non-Soc-L as their L1 and a Soc-L as their L2 in middle childhood.

2 Becoming Bilingual in Infancy: Focus on Bilingual First Language Acquisition

Infants may hear two languages from birth within the family. Infants may also be reared bilingually in spite of not living in a bilingual family. They may hear one language at home but may start to be regularly addressed in an L2 well before the second birthday, often through childcare outside the home, and are thus growing up in an ESLA setting. There are virtually no reports on ESLA *infants'* language development (but see Pavlovitch, 1920; Vihman, 1999). Hence the current section focuses exclusively on infants growing up with two languages from birth.

The section starts by examining what it means to be born into a bilingual family, and focuses on aspects of the language input to infants, that is, on what they hear. We know about input through written records kept by parents (often in the form of diaries), audio and/or video recordings, and parental questionnaires. Infants must learn to make sense of what they hear. How infants with bilingual input from birth do so is discussed in Section 2.2 on early speech perception. Most research here relies on ingenious experiments. Infants must learn to categorize sounds into units that are meaningful in each of their two languages. Learning how to do this is part of their phonological development, that is, the development of the sound system of a particular language. Section 2.3 goes on to describe the first steps in BFLA infants' word comprehension. Learning to understand words is part of infants' lexical development and has been studied through observation and sometimes experiments. The size of infants' comprehension vocabulary is assessed through parental questionnaires. The best known are the MacArthur-Bates Communicative Development Inventories (CDIs; Fenson et al., 1993) and their different language versions. CDIs were first developed in American English, but currently exist in about 50 languages and varieties (see the official CDI website).[7] CDIs are standardized report instruments asking caregivers to tick off on a list which words or phrases children understand and/or say. For children between 16 and 30 months, CDIs also ask about early word combinations. CDIs are important both in research and in clinical practice. For many languages CDI norms[8] have been established that allow clinicians to decide whether an individual child is developing as expected or not. BFLA infants' use of words and word combinations is the subject of Section 2.4. That section also discusses BFLA infants' phonological development in production.

Both in early comprehension and in production BFLA infants may develop each language at a different pace. This uneven development is the subject of Section 2.5. Section 2.6 examines factors that may influence early bilingual development in BFLA. A brief summary concludes Section 2.

---

[7] MacArthur-BatesCDI. (n.d.) [website] https://mb-cdi.stanford.edu/
[8] Vocabulary Norms. (n.d.). Word Bank [website]. http://wordbank.stanford.edu/analyses? name=vocab_norms

2.1 Born into a Bilingual Family

Once parents start talking to newborns, they may use both Language A and Language Alpha, creating a bilingual language input environment from the very start. BFLA newborns finding themselves in a bilingual family may hear each parent speak both languages to them. A second possibility is that one parent speaks both languages to newborns and the other parent(s) just a single language. Alternatively, each parent may address the newborn in just a single language (OPOL, the (in)famous "one person, one language" setting). The first two patterns occur about equally frequently; the OPOL pattern occurs least often (De Houwer, 2007; Yamamoto, 2001). Regardless of the language(s) parents use to address them, babies may overhear parents address each other in a third language (or more). The variation is large.

Language input patterns that infants experience from their parents are complemented by those from other people both inside (e.g., siblings) and outside (e.g., family friends) the home. Added to this variation comes variation in the number of people children come into regular contact with.

In addition to the variation in the languages BFLA babies are hearing and whom they are hearing them from, there is wide interindividual variation in how parents verbally engage with infants. Parents may speak to babies a lot, or less so. They may speak clearly, or less so. They may use a lot of typical infant-directed speech (IDS) with exaggerated intonation patterns, short utterances, and frequent repetitions, or less so. Listen to <u>excerpts of American English IDS</u>[9] that contain stimuli used for, among others, Byers-Heinlein et al. (2021). Listen to <u>typical Portuguese IDS</u>[10] (and young BFLA infant vocalizations) in the <u>Portuguese–Swedish MCF Corpus</u>[11] collected by Madalena Cruz-Ferreira (Cruz-Ferreira, 2006, is an in-depth study of the BFLA children featuring in this corpus). Parents may be verbally quite responsive to babies (illustrated in <u>this video of a father interacting with his infant</u>),[12] or less so. Parents may regularly read books and enact rhymes and songs with babies, or less so.

To what extent variability on parameters of parent–infant verbal engagement has to do with parents' bilingual status or with their status as being part of a bilingual or monolingual family has hardly been explored. Parents of bilingual and monolingual infants did not differ in the modalities of action, language, and

---

[9] Audio Stimuli. (n.d.). *Google Drive* [website]. https://drive.google.com/drive/u/0/folders/0B4NwkcR_udMNUmdOVzZVVkgtZFE

[10] https://media.talkbank.org/childes/Biling/MCF/Karin/020403.mp3

[11] MCF Bilingual Corpus. (n.d.). *Talkbank* [website]. https://childes.talkbank.org/access/Biling/MCF.html

[12] Acery [Screen name]. (2019, June 5) Dad Has Full Convo With Baby [Video]. *YouTube.* www.youtube.com/watch?v=0IaNR8YGdow

gesture during parent–child interaction with their 14-month-olds (Gampe et al., 2020). Mothers in bilingual and monolingual families addressed the same amount of speech to their 13- and 20-month-olds (De Houwer, 2014). However, within-group variability was large, with some monolingually reared infants having very silent mothers, and some bilingually reared infants having very talkative mothers, as well as the other way around (Orena et al., 2020, likewise found large variability among bilingual families in the number of words addressed to BFLA infants). Although it is often claimed that bilingual infants hear less of each language than monolinguals of their single one, the wide variability within each parent group as well as the lack of intergroup differences render this assumption doubtful (De Houwer, 2018b). Assumptions of bilingual–monolingual differences in frequency of input in a language are further complicated by possibly large variation within bilingual families in global use of a particular language, with parents speaking Language Alpha far more frequently during trips to the "home" country (Leopold, 1939–1949; Slavkov, 2015), or with families hosting grandparents who speak Language Alpha for weeks or months at a time (Leist-Villis, 2004). Such changes in environment directly affect the amount of speech that bilingual infants hear in each language.

Van de Weijer's (1997) acoustic study is unique in presenting analyses of intonation patterns in speech addressed to a BFLA infant and in comparing that IDS to adult-to-adult speech (ADS) by the same adults. Data were collected in the home for about 90% of the time that the Dutch–German infant was awake between 6 and 9 months of age (720 hours in total). A total of 4,376 utterances produced by mother, father, and a regular babysitter over a selection of 18 days were the basis for analysis. Compared to ADS, in IDS adults spoke much more slowly, used a much higher pitch, larger pitch variations, and more simple intonation contours that made utterance boundaries quite clear (van de Weijer, 1998, furnishes more details), confirming findings for adults in monolingual families. Van de Weijer's analyses did not focus on the family's bilingual nature. Focusing mainly on maternal speech, De Houwer (2009, pp. 121–123) analyzed information in van de Weijer (2000, 2002) about IDS to the infant and her sister, who was 2 years older. On average the mother spoke about twice as often to her toddler than to her infant, suggesting that IDS speaking rates of parents in bilingual families change as a function of children's ages, as was later confirmed in longitudinal studies of maternal speech to BFLA 13- and 20-month-olds (De Houwer, 2014; Song et al., 2012).

A study of language input within two days in the lives of 58 bilingual (at least 46 were likely BFLA) 10- to 12-month-olds in Paris found that many infants heard both French and one or more of 16 other languages within the same half-hour, rather than just a single language (Carbajal & Peperkamp, 2020). About half the families followed an OPOL approach. Regardless of parental input patterns, infants encountered more people who spoke French to them than their other language.

Parents in both bilingual and monolingual families may address infants in a language they themselves learned later in life. They may speak that language with a "foreign accent" (that is, an accent influenced by a language learned earlier in life). The chance that parents in bilingual families speak a language with a "foreign accent" is high. If they speak that language to infants, their use of IDS may show traces of a "foreign accent" as well. Fish et al. (2017) demonstrated how Spanish–English bilingual parents pronounced English words addressed to infants with both Spanish- and English-like characteristics. Fish et al. suggested that the use of specific bilingual characteristics of IDS may have implications for bilingual infants' early speech perception, the topic of the next section.

2.2 Phonological Development: Bilingual Infant Speech Perception

For bilingually reared infants to gain entry into each of the two languages they are hearing, they must be able to pay auditory attention to the way people verbally engage with them. Although BFLA infants can learn from any kind of language addressed to them, the special features of IDS capture infants' attention to speech. BFLA infants ($N = 333$) from various countries preferred to listen to IDS rather than to ADS (Byers-Heinlein et al., 2021). As Ronjat noted in 1913, BFLA infants not only use auditory but also visual cues as present on a speaker's face to help them process and distinguish the dual language input they receive (Weikum et al., 2007).

Newborns born into either bilingual or monolingual families are able to globally distinguish among languages (Byers-Heinlein et al., 2010). Languages differ widely in their use of particular sound patterns, that is, in their phonology. As part of phonological development, infants gradually learn to order the multitude of speech sounds they hear into perceptual categories that are relevant to the language(s) they are learning. They simultaneously learn to ignore perceptual differences that are of no consequence to meaning creation in the language(s) they are learning. BFLA infants must keep an "open ear," so to speak, toward a larger variety of speech sounds than monolinguals. They must develop sufficiently separate perceptual categories relevant to each input language to be able to learn words in each language.

Most words are independent units whose meaning relies on a particular combination of sounds. Languages differ widely in what kinds of sound patterns can form words and which are relevant to shaping word meaning. Most languages in the world use lexical tone, (i.e., pitch variations within the word unit) to help distinguish among words. For example, "ma" in Mandarin means <mother> if pronounced without pitch variation and <horse> if pronounced with falling and rising intonation. In non-tone languages like English and Dutch, words do not change meaning as a function of whether they are said in a monotone, with rising intonation, or with falling intonation: "ma" means <mother> in both Dutch and English regardless of the intonation pattern. BFLA infants acquiring non-tone languages hence do not need to pay attention to lexical tone (Liu & Kager, 2017). However, if one of the languages they hear relies on lexical tone for meaning distinctions, infants need to pay attention to word-level variations in pitch for that language (but not for a non-tone language they may be acquiring simultaneously). In learning new words, 12- to 13-month-old Mandarin–English infants relied on lexical tone in a Mandarin context but disregarded tone as a clue in an English context (Singh et al., 2016).

Words consist of one or more phones. Phones are speech sounds produced through one articulatory position. For example, "ma" consists of the phone [m], produced by closing the mouth and vibrating the vocal cords, followed by the phone [ɑ] or [a], produced by opening the mouth fairly widely and vibrating the vocal cords (the difference between [ɑ] and [a] depends on the position of tongue and lips). When the air flow from the vocal cords is constricted, people produce a consonant (like [m]); they form vowels (like [ɑ]) when the air flows freely (find out more about phones through this IPA vowel chart with audio).[13]

Languages differ in the type, number, and order of phones they use to make words. They also differ in the extent to which two phones contrast with each other. If they contrast with each other, the phones are phonemes. If they do not, they are allophones. Which phones contrast with which other ones depends on the language. Consider [w] and [v], both produced by pouting the lips a bit and vibrating the vocal cords. In [w] the air flow is fairly unimpeded. In [v] it is somewhat obstructed by tongue and lips. In German [w] and [v] do not represent a phonemic contrast but are allophones: When they are used in a word that is otherwise the same, there is no meaning difference. Thus, [wɪr] and [vɪr] sound the same in German: They mean "we" under either pronunciation. Infants learning German need not learn to distinguish between [w] and [v]. However, infants learning English do need to learn to distinguish between the two. That is

---

[13] IPA Vowel Chart With Audio. (n.d.). *Wikipedia* [website]. https://en.wikipedia.org/wiki/IPA_vowel_chart_with_audio

because using either creates a meaning difference: "a wet vet" is funny but "a vet wet" just doesn't make any sense (Germans will often fail to hear the difference). In English, [w] and [v] build the phonemic contrast /w/-/v/.

Learning to distinguish phonemic contrasts in each language is an important step toward deciphering the meanings of words. Studies of BFLA infants' speech perception in the first year of life have primarily focused on the early perception of consonant contrasts (Burns et al., 2007). Studies on the early perception of vowel contrasts (Sundara & Scutellaro, 2011) are rarer. Phonological perceptual learning continues well into the second year (Singh et al., 2017). There has also been attention to BFLA infants' perception of lexical stress, another feature that is differentially relevant depending on the language (Bijeljac-Babic et al., 2016).

Upon hearing utterances containing several words, infants need to learn where a word begins and ends. Statistical learning and perceiving overall pitch variations within an utterance likely play a large role in this process (Höhle et al., 2020). BFLA infants are able to distinguish both monosyllabic (Bosch et al., 2013) and bisyllabic (Polka et al., 2017) words in a speech stream well before the first birthday, and in some cases by 6 months. The growing literature on perceptual aspects of new word learning and familiar word recognition in the second year of life shows that BFLA children differ in the extent to which they use detailed phonetic information to process words, partly as a function of the specific contrasts investigated (Havy et al., 2016), and partly as a function of children's specific sensitivities to acoustic information (Fennell & Byers-Heinlein, 2014).

Even though the highly complex experimental research on BFLA infants' developmental paths in early speech perception is still quite "fragmentary" (Höhle et al., 2020), likely by the end of the first year BFLA infants will have learned to appropriately categorize some language-specific aspects of the phonological systems of the two languages they have been hearing. Whether this means infants are approaching their languages as separate phonological systems is, however, an open question (Höhle et al., 2020, and chapters 8 and 9 by Byers-Heinlein in Grosjean & Byers-Heinlein, 2018, offer more detailed treatments of bilingual infant speech perception).

Early speech perception abilities develop concurrently with infants' growing ability at interpreting contexts and people's communicative intentions. These combined abilities are the main basis for the emergence of early lexical comprehension. The ability to understand words has been experimentally documented for monolinguals as young as 6 months (Bergelson & Swingley, 2012). The next section discusses early language comprehension in BFLA infants.

2.3 Bilingual Infant Language Comprehension

Depending on the language pair BFLA infants are hearing, there may be a lot of overlap between words across both languages. Words that sound and mean the same across two languages are cognates. Parents talk about quite concrete things to infants that are relevant in both languages. Thus, infants also hear translation equivalents (TEs). TEs are words from each language that differ in form but mean more or less the same thing, such as Spanish "comida" and German "Essen" (food, eating). In contrast to TEs, infants may hear some things discussed only in a single language. For instance, if a father reads Turkish books about zoo animals with his Turkish–German son but the German-speaking mother does not mention animals, the child only has the chance to learn names for zoo animals in Turkish. In addition to the degree of lexical variation and overlap between languages A and Alpha the absolute number of words and the number of different words that BFLA infants hear in each language are likely different, with concomitant differences in relative exposure to words in each language (De Houwer, 2009).

The complex nature of BFLA infants' total lexical input may be seen as an arduous language learning environment. One might expect BFLA infants to take longer to start understanding new words and to build up their lexical comprehension repertoire more slowly than children growing up in a less variable, monolingual environment. One would therefore expect monolingual infants to have a larger comprehension vocabulary size than BFLA peers. So far, there is no evidence for slower bilingual development; in fact, there is evidence suggesting that a bilingual environment from birth boosts word comprehension.

The overall timing of first word comprehension by BFLA infants is no different from that reported for monolinguals (Clark, 1993). BFLA infants may understand words in both languages well before the first birthday. Three Portuguese–Swedish children first responded to their names at ages 4, 5, and 7 months (Cruz-Ferreira, 2006, p. 146). English–German Hildegard understood her name at 6 months, understood several English words by 8 months, and understood directions in both languages by 8 months (Leopold, 1939–1949). Cruz-Ferreira's (2006, pp. 146–147) Portuguese–Swedish children responded to simple commands at 7 months, and responded nonverbally but appropriately to routine questions such as "where is the clock?" by 8 months, thus showing some level of comprehension. Welsh–English 11-month-olds were able to recognize both Welsh and English words (Vihman et al., 2007). By the first birthday, BFLA infants routinely understand words in each of their languages.

Both clinical and research interest in early vocabulary size is great because of its strong relation with later language abilities (Bornstein & Haynes, 1998). BFLA average comprehension vocabulary size in one particular language does not differ from that of monolinguals. There were no differences among bilingual and monolingual infants (average age: 11 months) in the average number of French words understood (Carbajal & Peperkamp, 2020). Dutch–French first-born 13-month-olds ($N = 31$) understood as many Dutch words as 30 demographically matched Dutch-learning monolingual peers (De Houwer et al., 2014). Data collected for these same infants at 20 months likewise showed no bilingual–monolingual differences for Dutch comprehension vocabulary size. Rather, both ages showed large intragroup variability (De Houwer et al., 2014). The fact that studies comparing early comprehension vocabulary size for a single language found no bilingual–monolingual differences suggests that BFLA infants experience no particular difficulty in learning to understand new words.

We do find bilingual–monolingual differences when infants' total vocabulary sizes are compared. However, monolinguals perform far worse than bilinguals. BFLA infants' total vocabulary size includes both languages; monolinguals' vocabulary covers just a single language. On average, 13-month-old bilinguals in De Houwer et al. (2014) understood 60% more words than monolingual peers, with the top-performing bilingual understanding 564 words compared to just 358 understood by the best monolingual. Legacy et al. (2016) likewise found larger total comprehension vocabulary in 50 French–English infants aged 16 to 18 months compared to monolingual French-speaking peers, with bilinguals understanding 39% more words, and the top-performing bilingual understanding 693 words compared to the best monolingual's 387 words understood. In neither study were the best monolinguals performing at ceiling.

One factor driving BFLA infants' word learning may lie in TE comprehension. De Houwer et al. (2006) examined the understanding of 361 TE pairs across Dutch and French in the same 13-month-olds as studied in De Houwer et al. (2014). All infants understood TEs, words from two languages that meant the same thing (this does not imply that infants realized that one word was the translation of another). All infants also understood just single members of TE pairs. There was large interindividual variability in the number of TE pairs understood. Infants who understood more of the 361 meanings represented in the TE pairs compared to others tended to understand them in both Dutch and French rather than in just a single language. Learning to understand more words in early bilingual development thus appears to be (partly) connected with learning to understand the TE for an already known word. Legacy et al. (2016) similarly reported a correlation between comprehension vocabulary size and the proportion of TE pairs that their somewhat older sample understood.

We do not know how BFLA infants who understand (or produce, see Section 2.4.4) both members of a TE pair interpret each of these members, nor whether children understand that meanings overlap. Yet the term "conceptual vocabulary" (Pearson et al., 1993) is widely used not only in the research literature but also in clinical practice. It refers to vocabulary size counted in so-called "concepts," the number of lexicalized meanings that children know, abstracting from actual word forms across two languages in a TE pair (for monolingual children, "conceptual vocabulary" is identical with vocabulary size counted in words). To what extent such abstraction is valid is up for debate. However, studies comparing bilingual and monolingual infants' "conceptual vocabulary" comprehension sizes have found no intergroup differences (De Houwer et al., 2014; Legacy et al., 2016).

We know hardly anything about bilinguals' early semantic development, or about what drives this development. Experimental studies such as Byers-Heinlein's (2017) with 9- to 10-month-olds, Henderson and Scott's (2015) with 13-month-olds, and Kalashnikova et al.'s (2018) with 18- and 24-month-olds are starting to address some of the word-learning heuristics that bilingual infants use to learn to understand words.

2.4 Bilingual Infant Language Production

2.4.1 Babbling

Soon after BFLA infants start to understand words (or concurrently), they start to produce repeated syllables. Before the first birthday, these syllables consist of a consonant followed by a vowel. The use of repeated syllables by babies is known as babbling. When infants are a bit older they start to vary the syllables within one breath. Babbling appears to have little, if any, communicative intent.

Ronjat (1913) was the first to closely describe babbling in a BFLA infant and noted the importance of prosody (review in De Houwer, 2009, pp. 167–171). Ronjat did not discover any specific bilingual aspects of babbling, but in 1913 he did not have the technological tools for acoustic analyses that are available now. Such analyses showed that Spanish–English 12-month-olds used different prosodic patterns in babbling depending on whether they interacted with a Spanish or English interlocutor (Sundara et al., 2020). In doing so, infants reflected prosodic characteristics of, respectively, Spanish and English. These findings confirm earlier studies (Andruski et al., 2014; Maneva & Genesee, 2002).

Babbling is generally fairly short-lived, but there is wide variation among children in how long they continue to babble. Some BFLA infants stop babbling once they start saying their first "real" words, whereas others continue to babble. In order to communicate with others, words are crucial.

2.4.2 First Words

Early word comprehension predates early word production in most children. Toward the first birthday BFLA infants start to say syllables or combinations of syllables that parents identify as attempts at words (i.e., forms with a meaning attached to it). This BFLA milestone occurs around the same age as for monolinguals. Some BFLA (and monolingual) infants initially produce longish uninterpretable utterances with sentence-like intonation patterns concurrently with single word-like forms (listen to such uninterpretable utterances in this conversation).[14]

It is rarely clear what language BFLA infants' first words are aiming at. That is because the structure of children's first words is highly individual. However, there are commonalities across children and languages (Vihman, 2016).

2.4.3 Phonological Development: Learning to Produce Sounds

As they add words to their production repertoire, BFLA infants have to learn to use the appropriate sounds. Learning to use the right sounds entails selecting the correct consonant and vowel phonemes (Section 2.2) for each syllable, putting phonemes and syllables into an order that makes sense in a particular language, controlling one's voice to produce appropriate intonation patterns, and much more. All this pertains to the production side of phonological development. Phonological development in production is a long-drawn-out process that takes many years.

In comparison to adult pronunciations, both bilingual and monolingual infants delete or substitute sounds, shorten words, or repeat syllables. These phonological processes make it difficult to decide what word infants are trying to articulate. For BFLA children, phonological processes additionally make it hard to decide what language infants are using, and hamper attempts to decide whether children are developing language-specific phonological systems (the question of whether BFLA infants develop two separate linguistic systems has been of great interest to scholars).

As reviewed in De Houwer (2009), there is wide interindividual variation among BFLA children in the development of phonology. As children grow more mature and are better able to integrate what they know about how others

---

[14] Coldquads [Screen name]. (2013, October 3). Baby's Conversation with Grandmother [Video]. *YouTube.* www.youtube.com/watch?v=9gsjGAW18rk

speak and how they hear themselves speak, separate phonological systems may start to slowly emerge (Vihman, 2016).

2.4.4 Lexical Repertoire and Vocabulary Size

Not only does word comprehension predate word production, but like monolinguals, BFLA infants understand more words than they say (De Houwer, 2009). On average, 31 Dutch–French 13-month-olds understood 14 times as many words as they said (De Houwer et al., 2014). Whether the extent of this comprehension-production vocabulary gap persists is not known, but it is a common experience for people everywhere to understand more than they say.

By 12 months most BFLA (and monolingual) infants have started to speak. If there is no somewhat recognizable word production by this age, children's hearing should be checked. BFLA infants gradually start saying more different words (Porsché, 1983; Ronjat, 1913). Some bilinguals experience a vocabulary spurt: They suddenly start saying several new words every day. Others show a generally much more gradual increase in the number of different words said (Pearson & Fernández, 1994), but in all children an increase is expected. The average total number of different words that Dutch–French infants had in their production repertoire jumped from an average of 17 at 13 months to 254 at 20 months (De Houwer et al., 2014). Words come but also go again: Previously produced words may no longer be used. Patterns of bilingual early lexical development reflect those found in monolinguals, except that, according to CDI norms for several languages,[15] the total number of words that most 20-month-old monolinguals say is much lower than the average of 254 found in De Houwer et al. (2014).

There is extensive variation among infants in the speed with which they learn to say new words (and hence in their vocabulary size). Case studies show one BFLA child saying 100 words by 17 months, while another child did so only 3 months later (Vihman, 2016). The total number of words individual BFLA infants in De Houwer et al. (2014) produced varied between 0 and 82 at 13 months, and between 14 and 1,234 (!) words at 20 months. Legacy et al. (2018) reported similar ranges of variation. Cote and Bornstein (2014) reported narrower ranges for 20-month-olds (Spanish–English: 6–363, Japanese–English: 2–429, Korean–English: 13–590), but there was wide variation within each group. Notably, there is great variation among monolingual 20-month-olds as well (English: 4–487, Spanish: 1–402, Korean: 3–253, Cote & Bornstein, 2014;

---

[15] Vocabulary Norms. (n.d.). Word Bank [website]. http://wordbank.stanford.edu/analyses? name=vocab_norms

Dutch: 19–531, De Houwer et al., 2014; <u>CDI norms for monolinguals acquiring various languages</u> likewise show vast ranges of variation).[16]

Bilinguals may start saying words first in Language A, and only quite a bit later in Language Alpha. Not all BFLA infants produce words in both languages (13-month-olds, De Houwer et al., 2014; 15- to 19-month-olds; Legacy et al., 2018). Both these longitudinal studies found that all infants were producing words in both languages at the later age data were collected for (20 months [$N = 31$], De Houwer et al., 2014; between 20 and 26 months [$M = 24$ months, $N = 38$], Legacy et al., 2018). Bilinguals may also start saying words in both languages at the same time. After age 1.5 most BFLA infants say words in each of their languages (De Houwer, 2009). Children produce different numbers of words in each language (De Houwer & Bornstein, 2016a) and the gap between languages may widen with age (Legacy et al., 2018).

BFLA infants start producing TEs at different ages. They also differ in how many TEs they produce and in what proportion, relative to total production vocabulary size (David & Li, 2008; Pearson et al., 1995).

It is often claimed that bilingual children generally have a smaller vocabulary than monolinguals. So far there is no evidence to support this. Rather, CDI and CDI-like studies comparing production vocabulary size for young bilinguals and monolinguals have had mixed results. Because early lexical learning is very much linked to the cumulative number of words heard (Head Zauche et al., 2017), comparisons only make sense if the overall time for learning words has been equal. Hence the following brief review only considers studies of children with either bilingual or monolingual input from birth (because CDI studies may report on children up to around 2;6 (years;months), toddler findings are included here).

A first type of comparison considers children's total production vocabulary (always used as a basis for monolinguals). For bilinguals, this covers words in both languages combined. Studies failing to find any bilingual–monolingual differences are De Houwer et al. (2014; Dutch–French at 13 and 20 months), Pearson et al. (1993; Spanish–English, 16- to 27-month-olds), Legacy et al. (2018; French–English, 21–26 month-olds, $M = 24$ months), Hoff et al. (2012; Spanish–English; 22, 25, and 30-month-olds), Marchman et al. (2010; Spanish–English; $M = 30$ months), and Poulin-Dubois et al. (2013; French–English, 24-month-olds). When the French–English children in Legacy et al. (2018) were younger (15 to 19 months, $M = 17$ months), they produced more words than monolinguals. The total production vocabulary size of Spanish–Catalan infants

---

[16] Vocabulary Norms. (n.d.). Word Bank [website]. http://wordbank.stanford.edu/analyses?name=vocab_norms

between 12 and 24 months far exceeded that of monolinguals in either language (Águila et al., 2007). In contrast, Spanish–English 20-month-olds had smaller total vocabulary sizes (Cote & Bornstein, 2014).

A second type of bilingual–monolingual lexicon size comparison considers a single language for bilinguals (representing only part of their production abilities) and compares this single language with monolinguals' production vocabulary in the same language. Studies finding no differences include De Houwer et al. (2014; Dutch at 13 and 20 months), Legacy et al. (2018; French and English, $M = 17$ months; the language with the most words, $M = 24$ months), and Pearson et al. (1993; English between 16 and 27 months). In contrast to Pearson et al. (1993), Cote and Bornstein (2014), Hoff et al. (2012), and Marchman et al. (2010) reported smaller English vocabulary sizes for Spanish–English bilinguals (ages 20 months, 22, 25, and 30 months, and 30 months, respectively). Marchman et al. found the same for Spanish. The 24-month-olds in Legacy et al. (2018) did worse than monolinguals in the language bilinguals knew fewer words in. Poulin-Dubois et al. (2013) found that 2-year-olds speaking just English or French produced more English or French words, respectively, than bilinguals.

These mixed results for bilingual–monolingual production vocabulary size comparisons are likely attributable to: (i) the ages at which infants were compared to each other; (ii) the way parent report data were collected; (iii) differences among parent report instruments; (iv) whether studies compared raw scores or CDI norm percentiles; (v) the extent to which bilinguals and monolinguals were of similar socioeconomic status (see Section 5 below); and (vi) for single-language comparisons, the high variability among BFLA infants in the number of words produced in each language and whether studies made sure to consider only children's strongest language (see Section 2.5 below). Re (ii), for BFLA infants it is particularly important to get as comprehensive information on children's abilities as possible. Mothers whose children speak Language A to them but not Language Alpha will not be able to assess children's lexical repertoire in Language A. Thus, both researchers and clinicians should ask *all* regular caregivers to complete CDIs in the language(s) they address to children and/or children speak to them (De Houwer, 2019a).

Case studies (Cruz-Ferreira, 2006; Leopold, 1939–1949; Porsché, 1983) have traced some aspects of semantic development in BFLA infants (De Houwer, 2009), that is, about how children construct meanings and use words to express them. Holowka et al. (2002) investigated the lexical domains of three BFLA children's early words. However, we know very little about semantic aspects of BFLA infants' word use (DeAnda et al., 2016b). Research such as that by Jardak and Byers-Heinlein (2019) is sure to help change that.

2.4.5 Word Combinations

BFLA (and monolingual) infants' first words are usually produced in isolation (not as part of a longer utterance). These so-called "holophrases" often appear to express big meanings and several pragmatic functions. For instance, for several months German–English Nicolai used the form [das] to ask a question, confirm the correctness of something, express that he agreed with something, express excitement, and several other functions (Porsché, 1983). Eventually, BFLA infants start combining two words into a single utterance, as in "mamã peix" (mommy fish), said by a Portuguese–Swedish 20-month-old while her mother was drawing a fish (Cruz-Ferreira, 2006, p. 155). The earliest age reported is 15 months, but there is wide variation in the ages at which BFLA children start to combine words, as there is among monolinguals (De Houwer, 2009, p. 257; Patterson, 1998; Vihman, 2016). At any rate, the second half of the second year sees most BFLA (and monolingual) infants combining words. BFLA infants combine two words from Language A, two words from Language Alpha, or a word from each language. Utterances combining words from the same language are unilingual utterances. Utterances combining words from two languages are mixed utterances. Like first words, early two-word combinations do not necessarily appear in both languages at the same time (De Houwer, 2009; Lindquist & Gram Garmann, 2021).

The ability to combine two words into short utterances is a major milestone in early language development for bilinguals and monolinguals alike. If by the second birthday BFLA infants have not started combining words in at least one language, or in a mixed utterance, parents would do well to have children's hearing checked. Many BFLA infants are already able to produce short "real" sentences before the second birthday (De Houwer, 2009; see Section 3.1.2).

Production vocabulary size and word combinations are linked. BFLA infants say about a total of 50 different words before they start combining words, regardless of language (Patterson, 1998). Marchman et al. (2004) and Conboy and Thal (2006) found that the more English words bilingual infants (mostly BFLA, between about 1;6 and 2;6) produced, the longer their English utterances were. The same was true for Spanish. These relations between vocabulary size and utterance length held within each language, rather than across languages (see further Serratrice, 2019).

Word combinations increase the length of children's utterances. Utterance length is an important measure of early child language complexity and thus level of development. English–Spanish 17- to 30-month-olds ($M = 24$ months; $N = 113$; most of them BFLA children) were on average able to say equally long utterances in each of their languages, but there was large variability within each language (1 to 9 English words per utterance, $M = 2.3$; 1 to 7 for Spanish, $M = 2.6$; Marchman et al., 2004).

2.4.6 Language Choice

By age 1.5, BFLA infants produce words that do not clearly belong to a single language, either because they still sound too immature and it is impossible to say which language they are aiming at, or because there is lexical overlap between their two input languages. Children also produce words that clearly belong to Language A, and words that clearly belong to Language Alpha. For words that have a TE in the other language, children may say both members of the TE pair, or just one.

At any one time, bilinguals have to select among the words they know: They cannot pronounce two words at once. Bilinguals are not necessarily aware of which language they select, but language choice is not random (De Houwer, 2019b). BFLA infants' language choice is not random, either. From 1;6 onwards, BFLA infants often choose words and word combinations in the same language that their interlocutor speaks with them (De Houwer, 2009, pp. 141–145, 238–241). Infants are able to do so with both familiar (Köppe, 1996; Nicoladis, 1998; Sinka & Schelletter, 1998) and unfamiliar (Genesee et al., 1996) interlocutors. This ability may be related to BFLA infants' early ability to take another person's perspective (Liberman et al., 2017). However, BFLA infants do not always adjust to their interlocutor's language choice, and there are BFLA infants who hardly ever do (Section 2.6). For BFLA infants who are able to produce words in both Language A and Language Alpha, the "wrong" lexical choice may occur because they do not know a particular TE in the other language.

2.5 Uneven Bilingual Development in Infancy

Uneven development refers to cross-linguistic differences in the pace of bilingual children's language development and thus in their comparative proficiency in each language. Already at the earliest stages in comprehension BFLA infants do not necessarily develop each language at the same pace. Between ages 13 and 15 months, German–English Hildegard lost her prior ability to understand English and continued to understand only German (Leopold, 1939–1949). This occurred after her family had traveled to Germany from the United States when Hildegard was 11 months and she stopped hearing any English. It took two weeks after the family's return to the United States before Hildegard started understanding a few English words again (summary in De Houwer, 2009, p. 196). For some BFLA 12-month-olds, individual Spanish comprehension scores differed widely from those in English (Sundara et al., 2020, Appendix A). Only a small minority of 30 Dutch–French 13-month-olds understood about equal numbers of words in each language (De Houwer & Bornstein, 2016a). Most understood more words in one language than the other. Some infants in this sample understood many words in a single language but did not understand their translation in the other one (De Houwer et al., 2006).

Also in production BFLA infants may show cross-linguistic differences in the pace of development (Section 2.4.4). The timing of first word production in Language A may lag behind that in Language Alpha. Infants may say more words in Language A than in Language Alpha, or about equal numbers of words in each language. These balance patterns may be in flux over time. Two thirds of 30 Dutch–French BFLA infants showed a change in balance patterns for word production from age 13 to 20 months (De Houwer & Bornstein, 2016a). Six children showed a complete reversal and said more words in Language A at 13 months, but more words in Language Alpha 7 months later. Such drastic changes may help explain some of the mixed findings for bilingual–monolingual vocabulary size comparisons (Section 2.4.4).

Infants who understand more words in Language Alpha do not necessarily contemporaneously produce more words in that same language, or the other way around (De Houwer & Bornstein, 2016a). Both the changes that can occur in balance patterns for production and the fact that infants may show different balance patterns for comprehension and production suggest that speaking of "dominance" in a particular language as a general characteristic may be inappropriate. Uneven development also applies to word combinations (Section 2.4.5): Infants may be combining words in just a single language and not in the other.

2.6 Factors Affecting Bilingual Development in Infancy

There is great variability among BFLA infants in how they learn to process, understand, and speak two languages. An unsurprising reason lies in a child-internal factor, namely, in children's ages: Generally, the older they are, the higher infants' levels of performance on a particular language measure.

Perceptual abilities partly depend on age but differ among peers and underlie some of the variability among BFLA infants: Finnish–Russian infants who were comparatively better at discriminating a Finnish sound contrast at age 7 months had higher levels of both Finnish and Russian word production in the second year of life (Silvén et al., 2014). Garcia-Sierra et al. (2011) found similar results for Spanish–English infants. BFLA infants also differ in the speed with which they recognize words, and there likely is a bidirectional relation between the speed of online word processing and receptive vocabulary growth (Legacy et al., 2018). How well children are able to remember sounds (their phonological memory skill) affects both languages similarly (Parra et al., 2011).

Variability in early speech discrimination abilities may also be related to characteristics of the input. Orena and Polka (2019) focused on possible links between parents' use of mixed utterances (i.e., utterances with words from two languages, see Section 2.4.5) and bilingual development: The more parental mixed utterances 16 8-month-old and 20 10-month-old French–English infants heard, the better the infants were at segmenting bisyllabic words in either language, whereas infants whose parents reported using fewer mixed utterances tended to be good at segmenting words mainly in the language they heard more often.

Comprehension levels may also be affected by the input: BFLA 10- to 12-month-olds who heard two languages more often in the same half-hour block of time had lower French comprehension scores than BFLA peers whose language input in each language was more separated (Carbajal & Peperkamp, 2020). No such negative effects were found for the word production of older BFLA toddlers who frequently heard their languages within the same half-hour block, however (Place & Hoff, 2016). Instead, the proportion of the estimated time that BFLA infants hear each language can often help explain why children produce more words in one language than the other (Cote & Bornstein, 2014; David & Li, 2008; Legacy et al., 2018; Marchman et al., 2004; Pearson et al., 1997; Vila, 1984).

French–English infants' production of TEs across the second half of the second year correlated with changes in the proportion of exposure to each input language (David & Li, 2008). In contrast, for somewhat older French–English infants no such link was found (Poulin-Dubois et al., 2013). As De Houwer (2009, pp. 197–198) noted, "adults will often tell children what the translation equivalent of a word in Language A is in Language Alpha. They may do this by saying the words from each language one after the other." Parents may also actively engage infants by teaching them routines across different languages (watch how <u>parents are encouraging their 16-month-old's comprehension of words for the same things</u> in English and Spanish).[17] Variations in such TE teaching strategies may help account for variation in infants' TE comprehension and production.

---

[17] MisterO [Screen name]. (2011, October 23). Bilingual Language Acquisition [Video]. *YouTube*. www.youtube.com/watch?v=68rP2-ecPDM

However, research comparing observed parental engagement with infants in bilingual families and bilingual development is rare. Andruski et al. (2014) found that some aspects of bilingual babbling correlated with individual features of parental speech. Spanish–English bilinguals ($N = 18$; likely mostly BFLA) with greater exposure to IDS (Section 2.1) in English one-on-one parent–child interaction at ages 11 to 14 months had larger English vocabulary sizes at 24 months (Ramírez-Esparza et al., 2017). The same held for Spanish. The more bilinguals between 21 and 27 months were read aloud to in Spanish, the more Spanish words they were able to say (Patterson, 2002). The same was true for English. These effects were significant even when children's overall degree of exposure to each language was controlled for. Indeed, book reading can be of particular importance to BFLA infants' word learning (Cruz-Ferreira, 2006, pp. 182–184).

Finally, but importantly, parents socialize infants into (i) speaking only one particular language with them or (ii) speaking both languages or any language with them (Lanza, 1992). Parents do so through their discourse behavior in conversation. Infants may speak a language parents are not using with them in a particular conversation. In response, parents may use clarification requests ("Minimal Grasp Strategy") or requests for confirmation and/or correction as in "did you mean X?", where X is the translation of what the infant said ("Expressed Guess Strategy"). These monolingual discourse strategies encourage infants to repeat their original utterance in the other language and help to keep a conversation in a single language only. Parents may also simply repeat children's utterances in the other language. This "Adult Repetition" is neutral in terms of creating the need for the use of a particular language. Bilingual discourse strategies allow a conversation to take place in two languages. One is the "Move On Strategy," whereby parents just continue speaking the language they were speaking and do not interrupt the conversation after infants used another language. This conversational response signals to children that their language choice was fine. The second bilingual discourse strategy consists of parents themselves switching to the language infants used (Lanza, 1992).

Already in the second year of life BFLA infants are sensitive to their variable linguistic environment (De Houwer, 2017b) and to parental discourse strategies (De Houwer & Nakamura, accepted for publication 2021). Within a conversation, infants whose parents use mainly monolingual discourse strategies speak the same language that parents speak to them. Parents who use more bilingual discourse strategies tend to have infants who do not. If infants are not socialized into using a particular language, they may end up not speaking it. Parental discourse strategies thus have a very important role to play (De Houwer, 2009; see also Sections 3.6 and 4.6). In turn, infants may influence parental language choice patterns, to the extent that parents at least occasionally adapt to their infant's apparent preference (De Houwer & Bornstein, 2016b; Lindquist & Gram Garmann, 2021; Mishina, 1999) or give up speaking a particular language to infants (Eilers et al., 2006), thus following universal tendencies for interlocutors to accommodate to each other in conversation (De Houwer, 2019b).

2.7 Summary

By their first birthdays, BFLA infants have managed to sufficiently categorize the sounds they hear in each of their two input languages to be able to understand many words in each language. Many BFLA one-year-olds have also started to say a few words. Their vocabulary size in each language steadily grows throughout the second year, and when they reach their second birthdays, most BFLA children are able to combine words into sentence fragments. Many BFLA 2-year-olds are able to choose the expected language in speaking to parents.

BFLA infants' two languages do not necessarily develop at the same pace. The pace of development in each language relates to how often children hear each language and to their communicative need to actually speak two languages. This need is negotiated through parental socialization practices.

3 Bilingualism in Early Childhood: Bilingual First and Early Second Language Acquisition

As BFLA infants grow into toddlers and preschoolers, their world widens. This mostly happens through children enrolling in group childcare or more formal early education classes (henceforth: ECEC, Early Childhood Education and Care). As Sections 3.1 and 3.5 review, BFLA children's widening world has important effects on their bilingual development.

Many monolingual toddlers and preschoolers likewise enroll in ECEC. For a large proportion of monolingual children, such enrollment represents first regular contact with a second language (L2) if the main language spoken in ECEC is different from the L1 children hear at home. Children's language environment thus has changed to an Early Second Language Acquisition (ESLA) setting (Section 1). Section 3.2 describes ESLA children's early bilingual development.

Sections 3.1 and 3.2 both start with a discussion of children's developing language comprehension. Many studies rely on tests like the Peabody Picture Vocabulary Test (PPVT; Dunn & Dunn, 1997), currently available in several validated language versions (henceforth, the term PPVT refers to any language version of the original PPVT). Unlike the CDI (which is designed for younger children; see top of Section 2), the PPVT measures comprehension vocabulary size indirectly. Children have to pair a word they hear with one of four pictures they see. Only one picture is correct. Children's performance on the limited number of words queried through the PPVT is considered a proxy for children's overall comprehension vocabulary size. Standardized means established on the basis of test results from monolinguals are taken as the norm against which new test results are compared. Results of PPVT tests of young bilingual children are thus compared to monolingual-based norms (it is doubtful, however, that this is good practice; see, e.g., Haman et al., 2015). The available research often combines data from BFLA and ESLA children. Results are discussed in either Section 3.1 or Section 3.2 depending on whether most children in a study were likely BFLA or ESLA, respectively.

Discussion of children's comprehension is followed by an outline of language production in BFLA (Section 3.1.2) and ESLA (Section 3.2.2) toddlers and preschoolers. Information on young bilingual children's language production typically relies on observational studies employing parental diaries, labor-intensive transcriptions of audio recordings (with or without added video), or a combination of these. Many more such data are available for BFLA than for ESLA.

Section 3.3 compares the language development of BFLA and ESLA preschoolers and Section 3.4 discusses their language choice. Before the summary in Section 3.6, Section 3.5 explores both child-internal and child-external factors that may help account for patterns of bilingual development in early childhood.

3.1 BFLA Preschoolers' Language Development

3.1.1 Perception and Comprehension

Research on speech perception in BFLA children has mainly focused on infancy. What little research there is shows that in early childhood BFLA children continue to develop their speech perception abilities (Sundara et al., 2006). In contrast, there have been many studies trying to understand processes guiding BFLA preschoolers' comprehension of new words (Brojde et al., 2012; Yow & Markman, 2011). As with research on early BFLA speech perception, this body of work heavily relies on comparisons with monolinguals. For instance, monolingual preschoolers are strongly guided by the Mutual Exclusivity Constraint (MEC; Markman & Wachtel, 1988): When children already know the name for an object, they often reject a second name for it. In bilinguals a strong application of the MEC would block learning new words for the same object in another language. This does not happen: BFLA infants understand translation equivalents from early on (De Houwer et al., 2006;

Section 2.3). It is therefore not surprising that experimental research has found BFLA preschoolers' use of the MEC to be weaker than monolinguals', both for learning new object names (Davidson et al., 1997) and for learning new object property labels (Groba et al., 2019).

As for infants, there is limited research on BFLA toddlers' and preschoolers' comprehension vocabulary sizes. Smithson et al. (2014) found great interindividual variability among 77 French–English preschoolers' (a combination of BFLA and ESLA) comprehension scores on both the English and French PPVT. These bilingual children scored higher than the standardized means on both. Raw score comparisons with monolingual preschoolers acquiring either English or French found no bilingual–monolingual differences. Other studies with French–English preschoolers (mostly BFLA) equally failed to find any bilingual–monolingual PPVT differences (Comeau & Genesee, 2001; Sundara et al., 2006).

Although BFLA preschoolers continue to understand two languages, their level of comprehension in the Non-Soc-L may be much lower than that in the Soc-L (MacLeod et al., 2013), likely a direct effect of children hearing the Soc-L more frequently in ECEC (see further Section 3.5). BFLA children may show uneven development in comprehension already in infancy (Section 2.5), but in early childhood uneven development may become more pronounced.

3.1.2 Production

BFLA toddlers and preschoolers continue to use phonological processes (Section 2.4.3) that often make it hard to say which language they are speaking (Navarro et al., 1998). Although such phonological processes decrease with time, making it possible for unfamiliar strangers to understand most of what any four-year-old (bilingual or monolingual) says, phonological development continues over many years. Scholars have wondered to what extent BFLA toddlers and preschoolers construct separate phonological systems, and to what extent one language influences the other. Separate development is in evidence for some aspects, but less so for others (Marecka et al., 2020). Much depends on what is examined: phonemes (considered by themselves or in combination with one another; see Section 2.2) or prosody (intonation patterns on the lexical, phrase, clause, or sentence level). In addition, any findings are restricted by the limited number of language pairs-in-acquisition that have been studied.

As in infancy, BFLA toddlers and preschoolers produce translation equivalents (TEs). By age 2;6 (or even earlier), BFLA toddlers often spontaneously offer TEs, saying a word in Language A and immediately afterwards saying its translation in Language Alpha. Many are able to provide a TE on request (De Houwer, 2009). Such abilities show children's developing metalinguistic awareness, which appears to develop somewhat earlier in BFLA children than in monolinguals (De Houwer, 2017b). Translation abilities depend on children knowing the words for the same thing in each language. If BFLA toddlers exhibit large differences in production vocabulary size in each language (as found by Marchman et al., 2010; Hurtado et al., 2014; and Ribot & Hoff, 2014) the chance that they know TEs diminishes. The fact that BFLA toddlers have much larger production vocabularies in one language than the other also means they develop language-specific vocabularies from early on. As in infancy, this difference among languages is evidence of BFLA children's uneven development.

The few longitudinal studies of BFLA children's vocabulary development also show uneven development. A CDI study (top of Section 2) traced the growth of production vocabulary in 23 Russian–Finnish children from when they were infants (14 and 18 months) to when they were 24 and 36 months (Silvén et al., 2014). In infancy, Russian and Finnish vocabulary sizes kept pace with each other, but during early childhood Russian (the Non-Soc-L) vocabulary size stopped growing much, while Finnish (the Soc-L) vocabulary size grew quite quickly. Based on tests, Hoff and Ribot's (2017) longitudinal study found similar results for older children: From 30 to 60 months, BFLA preschoolers' Non-Soc-L scores (Spanish) were lower and increased far more slowly than Soc-L scores (English). The fact that the Soc-L developed faster was likely a direct effect of children attending ECEC in the Soc-L (see further Section 3.5).

In early childhood BFLA children greatly expand their speaking abilities. In this video you can hear 3.5-year-old Annabelle fluently speak German and Russian.[18] The short word combinations from late infancy have expanded into veritable sentences with four or five words. Sentences may contain appropriate inflection morphology (that is, parts of words attached to word roots that express grammatical meanings, such as plural -*s* marking in Spanish; see De Houwer, 2009, for deeper explanations) and different parts of speech, including function words such as pronouns and articles. Inflection morphology, function words, and word order constitute the main devices that languages of the world use to connect lexical roots with each other into sentences. These devices are known as morphosyntactic devices. Each language has its own range of morphosyntactic devices and its own rules for using them. Morphosyntax refers to

---

[18] Mama Nadia [Screen name]. (2020, August 21). Zweisprachige Kindererziehung: Klappt Das? || Tipps und Tricks für eine Bilinguale Erziehung [Video]. *YouTube*. www.youtube.com/watch? v=VSVHJp_KrJ8

the totality of devices that structure the combination of words in an utterance so that meaningful sentences are created.

The range of morphosyntactic devices that both bilingual and monolingual toddlers and preschoolers use is limited in comparison with adult uses, but continuously growing. By their third birthdays, many BFLA children produce long clauses and complex sentences consisting of a main clause and a subclause. By the time BFLA children are four years old, they can tell short stories, are usually fairly easy to understand for strangers, and have a large vocabulary (De Houwer, 2009). The global timeline here is similar to that for monolingual peers. As for monolinguals there is wide interindividual variability.

BFLA preschoolers also show cross-linguistic variability: For morphosyntax, BFLA children develop each of their languages independently of the other. In accordance with the Separate Development Hypothesis (De Houwer, 1990, 2009), BFLA children's unilingual utterances (i.e., with words from just a single language) use the morphosyntactic devices and rules of each of their languages separately: Utterances with words just from Language Alpha show a word order and use of bound morphemes and function words that fit Language Alpha (bound morphemes are grammatically meaningful sound(s) or syllable(s) attached to word roots; an example is -*ing* in English, which makes a gerund of verb roots such as *sing*). Utterances with words just from Language A show a word order and use of bound morphemes and function words that fit Language A. Morphosyntactic influence from one language on the other language is rare in BFLA and, if it occurs, is not systematic. Furthermore, BFLA children's unilingual utterances in each language are structurally very similar to those produced by monolingual peers (for mixed utterances, see Section 3.3). However, the main hallmark of children producing words and sentences is that children use them in conversations with others. The continued relevance and importance of conversations for children's speaking abilities is explained in Section 3.4.

Some BFLA children regularly produce mixed utterances (Section 2.4.5), whereas others produce none. On the whole, though, BFLA toddlers and preschoolers tend to produce unilingual rather than mixed utterances (De Houwer, 2009; Ribot & Hoff, 2014).

BFLA toddlers and preschoolers may not be equally proficient in each language. The language they speak less well usually is the Non-Soc-L (De Houwer, 2009). Many BFLA children even stop speaking the Non-Soc-L around age 4 or 5. This likely effect of attending ECEC in the Soc-L (Section 3.5) shows stark uneven development, with BFLA preschoolers continuing to understand two languages but speaking just one.

3.1.3 Summary

BFLA preschoolers continue to understand two languages. Many increase their production ability in each language, although one language can develop faster than the other, then slow down, and the other language can then "overtake" the first. Unilingual utterances in Language A show no systematic morphosyntactic influence from Language Alpha (nor the other way around). The morphosyntactic characteristics of utterances produced by BFLA preschoolers resemble those of monolinguals in the corresponding language. At the end of early childhood, BFLA preschoolers have high speaking abilities, often in two languages. By the time BFLA preschoolers enter school, they tend to speak the Soc-L better and at levels that are comparable to those of monolinguals speaking the same Soc-L as their single language.

3.2 ESLA Preschoolers' Language Development

3.2.1 Comprehension

When hitherto monolingual toddlers and preschoolers start to have regular contact with a new L2, they mostly encounter the L2 in group contexts, with only little supportive one-to-one child-directed speech (Jahreiß et al., 2018). For hitherto monolingual children, hearing structurally complex input in an unknown language in an unknown context first comes as a shock: Suddenly they can no longer understand what people are saying. This does not contribute to children's well-being (De Houwer, 2015b, 2020a): The first few months in an institutional environment in which ESLA toddlers and preschoolers do not understand anything can be an unpleasant, stressful, and even traumatic experience (Dahoun, 1995). Children may silently withdraw and disengage from interaction at preschool for months (Itoh & Hatch, 1978) or even years (Drury, 2007), resulting in an apparent rejection of the new language.

It will take some time before ESLA children start to pay attention to the new language and understand enough of it to correctly interpret what is being said. How long is difficult to say. Much depends on when children started to hear the new language and on a variety of other factors (Sections 3.5 and 6.2). ESLA children who regularly started hearing their L2 as of 2;8 showed a clear increase in L2 comprehension after a year (Schulz, 2013, and Korecky-Kröll et al., 2016, showed similar findings for somewhat older children).

Oral vocabulary learning is very much driven by how many words children have cumulatively heard (Head Zauche et al., 2017). Given that ESLA toddlers and preschoolers have heard their new L2 for a far shorter time compared to monolingual peers who have heard that language as their only language from birth, it is not surprising that bilingual–monolingual comparisons of L2-English comprehension have found ESLA preschoolers to lag behind monolingual peers (Bialystok et al., 2010).

3.2.2 Production

ESLA children who start regularly being addressed in an L2 soon after their second birthdays will be able to say many words in their L1 and will have started using word combinations and short sentences in their L1. The older ESLA children are when they first start regularly hearing the L2, the more advanced their L1 speaking skills will be.

After ESLA children have developed some level of L2 understanding, some gradually start to speak the L2 a little, but only in short formulae and in one- to two-word utterances (Itoh & Hatch, 1978). Other ESLA children soon start to speak the L2 a lot and quite well. Yet others do not speak the L2 even after 2 years (or longer) in preschool (Thompson, 2000). This "silent period" is often considered a "natural" and inevitable phenomenon of ESLA, but it is not. Young children who go through a very long "silent period" in the L2 are not doing well at a socio-emotional level (De Houwer, 2020a; Section 6.2).

Once ESLA preschoolers start to produce spontaneous utterances in the L2 that are not (partly) formulae or direct imitations, they may apply L1 morpho-syntactic rules in their L2 utterances. An example in L2-English is "I something eating," said by an L1-Turkish 4-year-old (Haznedar, 1997, p. 247), in which the child used Turkish word order. Such utterances showing clear morphosyntactic transfer (that is, influence from one language on the other) are to be expected in ESLA preschoolers (Li Wei, 2011; Pfaff, 1994; Zdorenko & Paradis, 2007). The proportion of such sentences compared to the totality of early L2 production is not known, but appears to be frequent and systematic within a limited learning phase (Schwartz et al., 2015). Inappropriately missing function words in the L2 can also point to transfer from the L1 (Blom, 2010; Reich, 2009; Rothweiler, 2016). Conversely, the new L2 can influence morphosyntactic phenomena in the L1 (Gagarina & Klassert, 2018).

In phonology, transfer from L1 to L2 is common in ESLA preschoolers (Babatsouli & Ball, 2020). Many ESLA children eventually speak without the "foreign accent" that is the result of such transfer, though.

Forms showing transfer or errors may persist as children grow older or may be replaced by the "correct" forms as children gain expertise in their L2. There is, unfortunately, little research on ESLA preschoolers' language development into the school years. We do know there is extremely large interindividual variation in the speed with which ESLA toddlers and preschoolers develop their new L2 (Hammer et al., 2012; Thompson, 2000; Winsler et al., 2014b). This variation makes it difficult to assess whether children are following a "normal" course of bilingual development. To make a proper assessment, children should be evaluated in both their L1 and their L2 (De Houwer, 2018a). A problem is that we know very little about the course of L1 development in ESLA toddlers and preschoolers who have started to regularly hear an L2. Most ESLA preschoolers likely continue to speak their L1. However, we know little about how well older ESLA preschoolers are able to speak their L1 after they have started to speak their L2. Reich's (2009) unique longitudinal study of 36 ESLA preschoolers who started hearing L2-German around the third birthday found that up to the fourth birthday most children gradually improved their speaking abilities in both the L1 and the L2, with increasingly complex sentences in both. At first, the L2 was less well developed than the L1. This changed in the fifth year of life, when for several children the L2 became significantly better developed than the L1.

As an example of an ESLA preschooler, listen to Petra. She started learning Mandarin after moving to China with her parents from the United States at age 2. After 14 months she started to speak some Mandarin, but with reluctance, at least in this video,[19] in which she also speaks some English, one of her first languages (Petra likely is both a BFLA and an ESLA child). One year hence, after 2.5 years in China, Petra learned to speak Mandarin fluently[20] and was able to communicate well and easily in various circumstances.

Uneven development is strongly present in ESLA, particularly at the first stages of L2 development: ESLA toddlers and preschoolers have already learned to speak their L1 to some extent but are just starting to acquire their L2. At first, their Non-Soc-L is far better developed than the Soc-L. Studies have explicitly addressed uneven development for lexical comprehension (Ertanir et al., 2018) and production (Budde-Spengler et al., 2018; Ertanir et al., 2018; Rinker et al., 2017). Older ESLA preschoolers may show larger comprehension and production vocabulary in the Soc-L than in the Non-Soc-L (Kan & Kohnert, 2005). This may be indicative of L1 speaking skills starting to stagnate.

3.2.3 Summary

ESLA toddlers and preschoolers understand and speak their L1 (a Non-Soc-L). Only very gradually do they learn to understand and speak a new L2 (the Soc-

---

[19] Real Life Cinema. [Screen name]. (May 28, 2013). American Child Learning Chinese Natively [Video]. *YouTube*. www.youtube.com/watch?v=026h0X0lD6I

[20] Real Life Cinema. [Screen name]. (June 16, 2014). American Child Speaking Fluent Chinese Mandarin [Video]. *YouTube*. www.youtube.com/watch?v=xbiqxkoLiO8

L), although some ESLA preschoolers may learn the L2 quite fast. By the time ESLA preschoolers enter school, many speak the Soc-L quite well, but many others do not. ESLA preschoolers' proficiency in the L1 may continue to develop but it may also stagnate.

3.3 BFLA and ESLA Preschoolers Compared

Sections 3.1 and 3.2 revealed some major differences between BFLA and ESLA toddlers and preschoolers. The differences in their cumulative linguistic experience first of all affect language comprehension. BFLA children have learned to understand two different languages simultaneously from the start. By the time they enter ECEC, they understand hundreds, if not thousands, of words in two languages. In contrast, ESLA children have no experience with people speaking different languages and can understand only a single language once they enter ECEC. This parallels the monolingual experience. ESLA children have yet to start learning to understand L2 words once L2 input starts. This has obvious implications for the comprehension of larger structures. A rare experimental study comparing bilingual children's sentence comprehension revealed that ESLA preschoolers performed far worse in German, their L2, than BFLA peers who had heard German from birth (Roesch & Chondrogianni, 2016).

Differences in BFLA and ESLA toddlers and preschoolers' overall linguistic experience also affect language production. By the time they enroll in ECEC, BFLA children can usually speak two languages. ESLA children start off speaking only a single language and may only very gradually start to speak another language (some children are faster). This difference in timing is particularly relevant for the Soc-L (ESLA children's L2, BFLA children's Language A). Even if BFLA children are performing better in the Non-Soc-L than the Soc-L before they start in ECEC, they speak the Soc-L much better than ESLA preschoolers do. BFLA toddlers' and preschoolers' attending ECEC in the Soc-L will soon lead to increased speaking ability in the Soc-L. In contrast, it may take ESLA children several months or longer to start speaking the Soc-L. Once they do, they initially perform much worse in the Soc-L than BFLA peers. In a rare direct (albeit numerically small) comparison, Dicataldo and Roch (2020) showed this to be the case for 28 bilingual preschoolers aged between 4 and 6. BFLA children in this group had heard the Soc-L, Italian, from birth and were doing far better on various Italian verbal tasks than ESLA peers who were acquiring Italian as an L2.

Once ESLA preschoolers are able to produce Soc-L sentences their morphosyntactic structures often differ from those that BFLA children use in the Soc-L. BFLA children's Soc-L sentences show no systematic influence from the Non-Soc-L (Section 3.1.2). In contrast, transfer from the Non-Soc-L is common in ESLA preschoolers' sentences in the Soc-L (Section 3.2.2). ESLA preschoolers may also use Soc-L sentence formation patterns that do not show a direct Non-Soc-L influence but that differ from patterns used by BFLA and monolingual children who have heard the Soc-L from birth (Granfeldt et al., 2007). A rare detailed comparison of French morphosyntactic structures as used by BFLA and ESLA German–French preschoolers showed that in L2-French, ESLA children made errors that BFLA children did not (Meisel, 2008). In the first few years of speaking the Soc-L, many ESLA children have a "foreign accent," which BFLA children do not.

The Non-Soc-L may also exhibit major differences among BFLA and ESLA children: many BFLA preschoolers no longer speak the Non-Soc-L. This has rarely been reported for ESLA preschoolers.

There are also similarities between BFLA and ESLA children in early childhood. Two-year-old BFLA (Ronjat, 1913) and ESLA (Idiazábal, 1984) toddlers may comment on who speaks what language. Spontaneously offering a translation equivalent for a word has been noted for both BFLA (Section 3.1.2) and ESLA (Idiazábal, 1984) toddlers. In both BFLA and ESLA preschoolers, mixed utterances mostly concern the embedding of a single free morpheme (mostly a noun) of language X in a statement in language Y (Cantone, 2007; De Houwer, 2009; Paradis & Nocoladis, 2007; Reich, 2009). BFLA and ESLA preschoolers' language choice patterns show both similarities and differences (Section 3.4).

Both BFLA and ESLA children may refer to some things only in one language (Rinker et al., 2017). Indeed, like this lexical usage, uneven development characterizes most BFLA and ESLA preschoolers' bilingual skills. However, BFLA preschoolers usually know the Soc-L better, whereas ESLA preschoolers usually know the Non-Soc-L better.

3.4 Language Choice in Early Childhood

BFLA toddlers and preschoolers usually select each language as a function of their interlocutor, addressing persons who speak Language Alpha with them in Language Alpha, and persons who speak Language A with them in Language A. However, with adults who they can expect to understand both languages, children may speak both languages, even if adults usually address them in just a single language (De Houwer, 1990; Paradis & Nicoladis, 2007; Ribot et al., 2018; Tare & Gelman, 2010). Ribot and Hoff (2014) showed 2.5-year-olds using different patterns of language choice depending on which language parents spoke to them. Children showed a preference for the Soc-L: When parents addressed children in the Non-Soc-L, children were more likely to respond in the Soc-L than the other way around (children were less likely to respond in the Non-Soc-L after parents addressed them in the Soc-L). BFLA toddlers and preschoolers may also speak *only* the Soc-L to parents, even if parents always address them in the Non-Soc-L (De Houwer, 2009; Eilers et al., 2006). Even if they occasionally speak the Non-Soc-L with people outside the family, children may soon lose the ability to do so. Non-Soc-L loss in early BFLA is not unusual, at least in production (De Houwer, 2017c). Thus, language choice in interaction helps explain uneven development: If young children do not regularly speak a language, they may lose the ability to use it.

Uneven development also affects language choice: You cannot speak the "right" language with someone if you don't speak their language. When ESLA children first start hearing an unknown L2 in ECEC, they usually remain silent rather than attempt to speak their L1. As soon as they can speak the L2 a bit, they mostly speak the L2 in ECEC, and the L1 at home (Reich, 2009). However, some ESLA children may start using the L2 at home, even though their parents do not speak it to them. If parents do not use monolingual discourse strategies (Sections 2.6 and 3.5), even ESLA preschoolers may lose the ability to speak their L1 (Kaufman & Aronoff, 1991; Lindquist & Gram Garmann, 2021).

When children are able to speak two languages they can switch between them without hesitations and basically speak the language that is spoken to them (this video with nearly 5-year-old Spanish–English BFLA Liam shows an example of this; Liam is the same boy as in the video referenced in Section 2.6 earlier).[21] Bilingual children are also able to repair their language choice upon request. Such responsiveness to interlocutors is only possible if children are sensitive to other people (Gampe et al., 2019).

This video[22] illustrates some dynamics of language choice in child–adult interaction when children speak two (or more) languages. About 30 seconds into it, 4-year-old Emi shows an English-speaking adult (likely her mother) a pink toy couch. She calls the toy a "divan," which is the correct Russian word. Her mother does not confirm that Emi has correctly described the toy, but briefly interrupts the exchange by saying the English word "sofa?" in a questioning tone. This use of this monolingual strategy, the Expressed Guess Strategy

---

[21] MisterO. (2015, June 3). Bilingual Development Update (Long Overdue)[Video]. *YouTube.* www.youtube.com/watch?v=T361-N1i3Dk

[22] 13ruskie [Screen name]. (2012, October 3). 4 Year Old Girl Speaks 3 Languages [Video]. *YouTube.* www.youtube.com/watch?v=jATItFipzBg

(Section 2.6), signals a confirmation query. In response, Emi quickly repairs her earlier language choice by switching to English and says, nodding: "yeah yeah, sofa," after which she continues in English. A bit later the mother speaks Russian with Emi, and Emi responds in Russian. At around minute 2:32, Emi compares a toy table to a piano, saying in English: "It's like a piano," but signaling nonverbally that she is not quite serious. Her mother chuckles and repeats in a light-hearted tone "It's like a piano?", after which Emi's face shows satisfaction that her little joke was successful. After this little aside she continues in Russian again. This example shows that briefly switching to another language can serve a pragmatic function. When in the Russian conversation Emi refers to the pink couch as "divan" (minute 2:44), her mother this time repeats the word in Russian with an admiring tone and makes confirmatory noises. Emi, appropriately, does not repair anything after that but just continues talking about the couch (in Russian). In the mostly Spanish conversation with a male adult that follows, Emi speaks Spanish, but both adult and Emi occasionally use a mixed utterance, inserting an English word into a Spanish utterance, thus adjusting to each other.

3.5 Factors Affecting Bilingual Development in Early Childhood

Children learn language through engagement with others. In bilingual settings, children's engagement with others is always linked to patterns of language choice as used by children's interlocutors. As was the case in infancy, the dynamics of language choice in parent–child interaction are crucial in helping to ensure that toddlers and preschoolers speak both languages. BFLA children who had been fluently speaking the Non-Soc-L to a parent may suddenly stop speaking it. This often happens after children come home from their first day in a Soc-L-speaking preschool (De Houwer, 2009, 2017c, 2020b). ESLA children may also bring the Soc-L home (Section 3.4). Parents can turn this tide through the sensitive use of monolingual discourse strategies (Section 2.6). Parental discourse strategies and language choices encouraging children to use the Non-Soc-L in conversations with them remain greatly important throughout childhood (De Houwer & Nakamura, accepted for publication 2021).

Children need many hours of using and thus practicing a language to become expert speakers (Clark, 2003; Hurtado et al., 2014). Ribot et al. (2018) showed that BFLA preschoolers who spoke the Soc-L more often spoke it better. Conversely, less or no use of the Non-Soc-L by children who are not yet fluent speakers may lead to language loss (at least in production). This downward spiral may be exacerbated by Non-Soc-L-speaking parents switching to the Soc-L with children, resulting in diminished input in the Non-Soc-L. As outlined in Section 3.5.2, continued rich exposure to both languages is important for BFLA and ESLA alike.

Basic differences among BFLA and ESLA preschoolers in Soc-L skills relate to the fact that BFLA children have heard the Soc-L from birth whereas ESLA children have not: ESLA preschoolers simply have had less time to learn it. Thus, it is not surprising that German–Turkish BFLA toddlers up to 30 months of age produced many more German words than ESLA peers who only heard L1-Turkish at home (Budde-Spengler et al., 2018). Length of exposure was a major factor in older BFLA and ESLA preschoolers' German word comprehension and production (Vaahtoranta et al., 2020). The story is of course more complicated: BFLA and ESLA children are also at different developmental stages when they first start to regularly hear the Soc-L. Additionally, when BFLA infants first start to hear the Soc-L, they know very little about language, but ESLA toddlers and preschoolers already know quite a bit.

The factors affecting the course of bilingual development are multiple, complex, and dynamically interact with each other (Hammer et al., 2012). They include factors particular to children as growing individuals (known as child-internal factors) and factors relating to the environments in which children are growing up (child-external factors). Child-internal and child-external factors are closely linked, and disentangling them is a challenge (Chondrogianni & Marinis, 2011; Sun et al., 2020). Many studies have examined factors that may help explain bilingual development. These studies usually do not focus on individual developmental trajectories but aim to explain intragroup variability. The remainder of this section is a highly selective review (for more details, see Armon-Lotem & Meir, 2019, and De Houwer, 2018b).

3.5.1 Child-Internal Factors Affecting Bilingual Development in Early Childhood

The most obvious child-internal factor is chronological age (see also Section 2.6). Age is a proxy for increases in cumulative language exposure, cognitive maturity, memory skills, interactional skills, and much more. Unsurprisingly, older children typically have higher developed language skills than younger ones. Studies focusing on internal factors have mostly concentrated on ESLA children.

Not unexpectedly, L2 vocabulary size and morphology are better developed in older than younger ESLA preschoolers; children's phonological short-term memory and nonverbal intelligence are also strong predictors (Paradis, 2011; phonological short-term memory refers to children's ability to keep sounds buffered in short-term memory). ESLA preschoolers' phonological memory abilities are related to both L1 and L2 vocabulary size (Ertanir et al., 2018). Furthermore, ESLA differences in children's early socio-emotional competence help predict their L2 learning (Ertanir et al., 2019; Winsler et al., 2014b), as does personality: Shy ESLA preschoolers take longer to start speaking the new L2 (Keller et al., 2013; Reich, 2009), whereas children who are eager to learn the new L2 and ready to engage with peers develop it faster (Schwartz et al., 2020).

A child-internal factor specific to bilinguals concerns their knowledge of the other language. The greater ESLA children's L1-Spanish vocabulary size was at age 2, the better they scored on L2-English comprehension and production measures 2.5 years later (Marchman et al., 2020). This longitudinal relation was partly moderated by toddlers' efficiency at processing Spanish words at age 2. The supporting role of ESLA children's L1 for later L2 development has also been found for older children: The better developed L1-Spanish was at age 4, the faster ESLA preschoolers acquired L2-English a year later (Winsler et al., 2014b). Confirming similar results from earlier studies involving different language pairs in different countries, ESLA preschoolers' L1-Turkish comprehension vocabulary size predicted L2-Dutch comprehension vocabulary size (Sierens et al., 2019). In contrast, neither in ESLA (Ertanir et al., 2018) nor in BFLA (Marchman et al., 2010) did production vocabulary size in one language concurrently predict production vocabulary size in the other. However, Marchman et al. (2010) found strong concurrent within-language links between BFLA toddlers' ability to understand familiar words in a lexical processing task, on the one hand, and production vocabulary size, on the other; children's processing speed in Language Alpha did not correlate with Language A vocabulary size (see also Hurtado et al., 2014). BFLA 30-month-olds who produced more Spanish than English words as rated through the CDI (top of Section 2) had higher Spanish than English PPVT-based comprehension scores 6 months later (Hurtado et al., 2014). Furthermore, Hurtado et al. (2014) found strong within-language links between these 3-year-olds' real-time word processing abilities and comprehension as measured by the PPVT. In addition, there were significant correlations between children's relative exposure to Spanish vs. English and their relative speed of processing of Spanish vs. English words. Thus, even for an internal characteristic such as processing ability, external factors play a role. Palacios et al. (2015) showed how a child-internal factor (level of language development) was dynamically influenced by an external factor, namely, parental interaction: Spanish–English bilingual children's different levels of language development elicited different levels of supportive language input from parents, which in turn affected children's linguistic skills.

3.5.2 Child-External Factors Affecting Bilingual Development in Early Childhood

As indicated just before Section 3.5.1, differences between BFLA and ESLA children's development in the Soc-L can (partly) be attributed to differences in cumulative amount of input. Amount of input plays a fundamental role in other ways as well.

As for infants, the relative amount of input in each language helps explain why BFLA toddlers and preschoolers have a better command of Language A than Language Alpha: The language that is heard more often is the one that is better developed. This has been shown for growth in comprehension vocabulary (Scheele et al., 2010) and production vocabulary size (Marchman et al., 2010; Nakamura & Quay, 2012; Place & Hoff, 2011) as well as grammatical development (Blom, 2010; Hoff et al., 2012). ESLA preschoolers' levels of comprehension and production in each language likewise related to the concurrent relative amount of input in each language (Marchman et al., 2020).

However, even though Finnish–Swedish BFLA toddlers and preschoolers in Silvén et al. (2014) heard the Non-Soc-L (Finnish) more often, the Non-Soc-L did not develop as fast as the Soc-L (Swedish). Silvén et al. (2014) attributed the Non-Soc-L's slower development to children becoming more involved with caregivers and peers outside the home who spoke the Soc-L as they grew older. Additionally, school-aged bilinguals may foster their younger bilingual preschool-aged siblings' learning and appreciation of the Soc-L through play and literacy-based activities in the Soc-L (Kibler et al., 2014; Mirvahedi & Cavallaro, 2020). You can see an example of how older siblings bring the Soc-L into the home through play-school activities starting at about minute 3:40 in this French–Dutch video.[23] Families that do not send their preschoolers to ECEC stand a greater chance of having children who speak the Non-Soc-L (Verdon et al., 2014).

In addition to children hearing unilingual utterances, they may also hear mixed utterances (which combine words from two languages; see Section 2.4.5). Often, people have negative attitudes toward the use of mixed utterances (De Houwer, 2019b). One might worry that hearing mixed utterances negatively affects children's bilingual development. So far, there is no evidence that they do (Place & Hoff, 2016).

One language may be heard more often than another, but absolute amount of input may be low in both languages, or high. Does this difference matter? Marchman et al.'s (2017) study suggests that it does: Absolute measures

---

[23] HaBilNet [Screen name]. (2017, September 26). Les enfants bilingues [Video]. *YouTube*. www.youtube.com/watch?v=qJ9Uihrqx2A

tallying the actual number of Spanish and English words addressed to 3-year-old bilinguals (likely a mix of BFLA and very early ESLA children) far better predicted children's language outcomes in each language than relative measures. As was the case for adults addressing BFLA infants (Section 2.1), Marchman et al. (2017) found large variability in the amount of adult speech to preschoolers.

Typically, the language spoken by staff in ECEC is a variety of the local Soc-L. Staff generally do not understand, let alone speak, whatever Non-Soc-L BFLA and ESLA children have learned to understand and speak. BFLA children in ECEC will likely hear the Soc-L more often than they did before they were attending ECEC. This increased absolute amount of input is likely partly responsible for BFLA preschoolers' relatively greater proficiency in the Soc-L in the preschool years (compared to the Non-Soc-L). At the same time, the hours spent in ECEC diminish opportunities to hear and speak the Non-Soc-L. This decreased absolute amount of input is likely partly responsible for many BFLA preschoolers' slower development in the Non-Soc-L in the preschool years (compared to the Soc-L).

Absolute amount of input is also important in ESLA: A longitudinal study of preschoolers with L1-Turkish and L2-German found faster L2 comprehension vocabulary development in children who spent more time at a German preschool, and thus had higher amounts of L2 input (Czinglar et al., 2017). This effect was independent of the length of time children had spent at preschool, although as in Blom and Paradis (2015) the overall duration of L2 contact was also an explanatory factor, with children who started attending preschool earlier having better L2 skills. Methods developed for assessing possible L2-German delays in preschoolers take into account length of contact with the L2 (Schulz & Tracy, 2011).

However, as in infancy (Section 2.1) there can be no assumption of stable comparative levels of input in each language throughout bilingual children's early language learning years. The absolute amount of input in a particular language is highly variable over time, and affects relative amount of input. This variability makes it hard to correctly evaluate bilingual input environments.

In addition to addressing children in the Non-Soc-L, parents may start speaking the Soc-L to them once children start attending preschool, thus leading to decreased input in the Non-Soc-L. A longitudinal study reporting on a mix of BFLA and ESLA preschoolers showed that the average percentage of Non-Soc-L input to children decreased from 66% when children were 2.5 to 58% when children were 5 years old (Lauro et al., 2020). Parents usually start speaking the Soc-L to children in response to children addressing parents in the Soc-L (Kuo, 1974; Luo et al., 2020; Prevoo et al., 2011). The fact that children no longer want to speak the Non-Soc-L may be the result of children developing negative attitudes toward the Non-Soc-L (a child-internal factor), which, in turn, may have been shaped by negative experiences in ECEC. ESLA children who do not yet speak the Soc-L well may experience bullying by peers (shown by Chang et al., 2007, in the United States and by von Grünigen et al., 2012, in Switzerland), which helps deliver the message that children need to focus on quickly improving their Soc-L skills, and forget the Non-Soc-L. Because BFLA children's Non-Soc-L is usually ignored at preschool, BFLA preschoolers may soon learn that the Soc-L is socially more important (De Houwer, 2015b, 2020b) and turn against the Non-Soc-L.

Whereas one expects increased or decreased input in language X to affect children's use of language X, there is no expectation that input in language X directly affects language Y. Yet Willard et al. (2021) found exactly this to be the case: Parental literacy activities in a Non-Soc-L contributed to ESLA children's comprehension of the Soc-L. Children's language experience thus must be considered holistically.

Yet on a more detailed level, the kind of input (often called "input quality") to children may play a language-specific role. Bilingual parents may have unequal levels of proficiency in each language and thus may address children at variable proficiency levels (Hoff et al., 2020). These variable proficiency levels may affect children's language development: Preschoolers who heard the Soc-L (Dutch) from parents who spoke it well, regardless of whether parents spoke Dutch as an L1 or L2, did better in Dutch than children whose parents spoke Dutch less proficiently (Unsworth et al., 2019).

Young BFLA children's language use may show apparent and unexpected influence from the other language. Studies comparing such apparent influence from the other language in young BFLA children's language use with highly proficient bilingual parents' input showed that idiosyncrasies in parental input could account for children's language use (Bosch & Ramon-Casas, 2011; Meisel et al., 2011; Paradis & Navarro, 2003; but see Nakamura, 2015). Given that the actual speech that children hear is the basis for their language intake (De Houwer, 2017a), studies trying to explain unexpected patterns of bilingual development should include measures of actual speech to children. Only then will correct interpretations of children's language use be possible.

As stated at the top of this section, parental discourse strategies in response to children's language choice play a crucial role in creating a continued need for children to speak the Non-Soc-L. Absent this need, children may simply not speak the Non-Soc-L, regardless of how much they hear it or how well parents speak it.

3.6 Summary

BFLA and ESLA toddlers' and preschoolers' fundamentally different language-related experiences lead to different trajectories for language development in early childhood. Although there is great interindividual variability, the following generalizations can be made. Whereas BFLA children understand and speak two languages at the beginning of early childhood, ESLA children understand and speak just a single language (their Non-Soc-L). In the early childhood years, both BFLA and ESLA children make gains in their proficiency in the Soc-L, but even by the end of early childhood, BFLA children understand and speak the Soc-L at far higher levels than most ESLA children. Although many BFLA and ESLA preschoolers continue to understand and speak the Non-Soc-L at high levels, BFLA preschoolers are more at risk of losing the Non-Soc -L than are ESLA preschoolers. Both BFLA and ESLA preschoolers adjust their language choice to their interlocutors and are sensitive to the degree to which interlocutors socialize children into responding in the Non-Soc-L. Such language socialization efforts are crucial in supporting the Non-Soc-L. Further support for the Non-Soc-L comes from the amount of language input in the Non-Soc-L. Frequency of input also matters for the Soc-L.

4 Bilingualism in Middle Childhood: Bilingual First Language Acquisition, Early Second Language Acquisition, and Second Language Acquisition

The beginning of middle childhood coincides with many children starting to attend primary school. Section 4.1 describes aspects of BFLA and ESLA schoolchildren's bilingual development. Section 4.2 zooms in on Second Language Acquisition (SLA) children, namely, on hitherto monolingual schoolchildren who start hearing their new L2 at school, and who need to learn it from scratch. Section 4.3 explains how, as at earlier ages, bilingual schoolchildren show evidence of uneven development. Whenever bilingual children speak more than a single language, they must select a specific language in speaking. Language choice is the topic of Section 4.4. Before the brief summary in Section 4.6, Section 4.5 explores factors that can help explain bilingual development in middle childhood.

Unless otherwise specified, reference to schools in this section assumes that schools use only or mainly a single Soc-L as a vehicle of instruction. In these schools, children usually do not get much specific support to help them develop the Soc-L but are mostly in a "sink-or-swim" situation (Kim et al., 2015; note there is a range of educational approaches). This circumstance differs from many preschools, which often have programs in place to help ESLA children develop the new L2 through one-on-one supportive interaction with preschool staff.

4.1 BFLA and ESLA Schoolchildren's Language Development

Upon school entry, both bilingual and monolingual children still have a lot to learn in the Soc-L used at school (Pearson, 2019). BFLA children who have heard the Soc-L from birth will normally be well positioned to cumulatively learn the kind of language expected at school and can normally already speak the Soc-L well. In contrast, ESLA children who started learning the Soc-L in early childhood may as yet lack sufficient proficiency to be able to optimally function at school. Many ESLA children are likely to understand the Soc-L well enough to understand most of what is going on in school, but their speaking skills may as yet be underdeveloped.

Many BFLA schoolchildren are able to fluently speak two or more languages, although not necessarily at similar levels. In this video you can listen to a girl speaking Spanish, French, German, and English.[24] Like monolinguals, BFLA children have not, however, learned all the complexities of the sound systems of each of their languages yet. BFLA schoolchildren may show occasional influence from the other language in the production of certain sounds (Mayr & Montanari, 2015). Some studies have found signs of influence from the other language in morphosyntax as well (Argyri & Sorace, 2007; Serratrice, 2007), but there have been no reports of systematic transfer in BFLA schoolchildren. In middle childhood, the strong differential effects of BFLA and ESLA children's language learning trajectories on Soc-L morphosyntactic forms that were apparent in early childhood may start to level off (Gathercole & Thomas, 2009; Unsworth, 2013), largely because of older ESLA children's gains in the Soc-L. Research interest in the morphosyntactic features of ESLA schoolchildren's L1 is fairly new (Chondrogianni & Schwartz, 2020).

Uccelli and Páez (2007) traced production vocabulary and narrative development in both the L1 (Spanish, the Non-Soc-L) and the L2 (English, the Soc-L) in 24 mostly ESLA children from the first to the second school year. Children made strong gains in the L2 but, unsurprisingly, were not (yet) performing at English vocabulary levels normed for children with input to English from birth. Gains in the L1 were only seen in storytelling. A longitudinal study of likely both BFLA and ESLA children spanning 5 primary school years ($N = 139$) examined children's speed and accuracy on a timed picture-naming task in both

---

[24] Multilingual Education – Playing, Learning, Growing [Screen name]. (2016, October 30). Bilingualism and More – Switching: Spanish – French – German & English no accent | Switching Codes [Video]. *YouTube*. www.youtube.com/watch?v=cSy1490WSU0

Spanish and English (Oppenheim et al., 2020). In both languages, children improved with time. Both at group and individual levels, children performed better in the Non-Soc-L prior to around the eighth birthday, but afterwards the balance reversed, and children performed better in the Soc-L (English). Dubiel and Guilfoyle (2017) found similar results for L1-Polish children in Ireland. Aarssen (1996) did so for L1-Turkish children in the Netherlands. A study relying on processing rather than production measures demonstrated that not all ESLA children perform better in the L2 than the L1 after age 8: L1-Italian/L2-German ESLA 8.5-year-olds who had started hearing the L2 in preschool and were attending an Italian-German school performed much better in their L1 than their L2 on accuracy and speed in lexical judgment tasks (Persici et al., 2019).

Finally, in early childhood BFLA and ESLA children's mixed utterances mainly embedded a content word from language X into an utterance in language Y. To be able to produce more complex mixed utterances, better dual language skills may be necessary. Indeed, BFLA and ESLA Spanish–English schoolchildren with longer experience with both their languages produced more complex mixed utterances than just insertions of a single word or phrase (Zentella, 1997).

4.2 SLA Schoolchildren's Language Development

There are few detailed studies of the course of language development in schoolchildren who started hearing an L2 in middle childhood. Very little is known about the development of L2 comprehension in SLA schoolchildren. Uchikoshi (2006) showed that 150 children acquiring English as an L2 (a mix of ESLA and SLA children) made rapid gains in L2-English comprehension throughout the first school year, achieving the level of 4.5-year-old English monolinguals by the end of the first year of school. Whether that level is sufficient for full participation in school at the beginning of second grade is unclear. School test results from primary school children worldwide suggest that it may take a long time for SLA children to understand the L2 sufficiently to fully participate in school (UNESCO, 2016).

For production, and similarly to studies of ESLA toddlers and preschoolers, the few extant studies tend to focus on the L2. Wagner-Gough (1975) as partly reprinted in Hatch (1978) analyzed the very first L2-English utterances produced by Homer, who started speaking L2-English just a few weeks after arriving in the United States and enrolling in an English-speaking school, just before turning 6. He had an American 5-year-old friend right after his arrival. Homer first imitated English words and phrases and replied to yes/no-questions by repeating them without question intonation. In the second month, Homer went beyond imitations and started forming sentences of his own making. The Homer example shows that in SLA there need not be a prolonged "silent period" as experienced by so many younger ESLA children.

Itani-Adams et al. (2017) described a longitudinal case study of L1-English 7-year-old John learning L2-Japanese through immersion in a Japanese-medium school in Australia. John started attending school at 6;3. By age 7 he was producing many Japanese words with verbal inflection morphology. Soon after, phrasal morphology emerged and 4 months later inter-phrasal morphology. Two years after enrolling at school, John was able to use a variety of complex structures in L2-Japanese. Itani-Adams et al. compared John's L2 development with the development of Japanese as heard from birth by a BFLA toddler and preschooler with excellent age-appropriate speaking skills in both Japanese and English. After just 2 years of L2 input, John used much more advanced morphosyntactic structures than the BFLA preschooler with nearly 5 years of input in Japanese. Mobaraki et al. (2008) reported on two L1-Farsi siblings who started hearing L2-English at school after arriving in the United Kingdom at 7;3 and 8;3, respectively. Three months after arrival these children were producing multiword utterances in their L2, but they used some word orders that would have been fine in Farsi but are not English-like (as in "We tennis play", p. 220). These early structures are similar to structures showing morphosyntactic transfer in ESLA preschoolers (Section 3.2.2). Over the 20 months of observation, the siblings' English became gradually more English-like, and Farsi-like word orders in English disappeared. Pienemann (1981) studied the development of auxiliaries and pronouns in L2-German in two L1-Italian 8-year-olds who had just moved to Germany.

As in ESLA, there is great interindividual variability in the rates at which SLA schoolchildren learn to speak their L2. A longitudinal study of 89 SLA children found that some could speak L2-English well after just 1 year at school (MacSwan & Pray, 2005). Others needed 6.5 years to do so. Most (92%) children took 5 years to reach a high level of L2-English proficiency. Oller and Eilers' (2002) cross-sectional study largely confirmed this picture. A large longitudinal study of low-income children in the same bilingual area (Miami, Florida) found that 90% of children were considered proficient in English by third grade (Kim et al., 2014). This percentage likely covers data from BFLA, ESLA, and SLA children. Focusing on academic achievement, Collier and Thomas (2017) reported that it takes SLA schoolchildren in English-only instruction in the United States between 7 and 10 years to achieve age-appropriate levels across the English school curriculum and stay at that grade level (or better) throughout the rest of their schooling (the authors based their findings on their longitudinal studies involving millions (!) of children, from kindergarten through grade 12).

At the more detailed level of morphosyntax, Haberzettl et al. (2013) found differences in the pace with which SLA children learned to correctly order L2-German verbs and to use correct verb forms. Like MacSwan and Pray (2005), Haberzettl et al. (2013) found that the older SLA children were when they started learning the L2, the less time they needed to develop good L2 skills (recall that Itani-Adams et al. (2017) found much faster development of the same morphosyntactic structures in an older SLA than a younger BFLA child). The authors attributed this difference to greater cognitive maturity in older learners and to greater experience with learning an L1 (for more discussion of factors affecting bilingual development in middle childhood, see Section 4.5).

4.3 Uneven Bilingual Development in Middle Childhood

De Houwer (2007) found that 1,356 6- to 9-year-olds in dual-parent families in Flanders, Belgium, heard two languages from their parents at home. They can thus be considered to have grown up in a BFLA setting. Nearly a third (30.3%) spoke only the Soc-L (Dutch) and did not speak the Non-Soc-L that at least one of their parents spoke (see further Section 4.5). It is rare for ESLA or SLA students who only hear a Non-Soc-L at home not to speak it: only 3% of 422 6- to 9-year-olds who only heard a Non-Soc-L at home did not speak it (De Houwer, 2007). Summarizing surveys across the globe, De Houwer (2020b) found that one in four bilingually reared children did not speak one of the languages heard at home. Invariably, the language that children did not speak was a Non-Soc-L.

We know little about the comparative skills in each language of BFLA schoolchildren who speak two languages. Persici et al. (2019) found no cross-linguistic differences in Italian-German BFLA students' performance on a lexical judgment task. Many ESLA students perform better in the L1 than the L2 in the first years of school, only to see this picture reversed around their eighth birthdays (Section 4.1). SLA children are likely performing at a fairly high level in their L1 when they enter school at age 6 and start to learn a new L2 there. L1-Russian/L2-German SLA students self-reported that they spoke the L1 much better than the L2 (Ahrenholz et al., 2013). It remains to be investigated how SLA schoolchildren's L1 continues to evolve as they gain more proficiency in the L2.

4.4 Language Choice in Middle Childhood

BFLA schoolchildren who speak two languages are able to easily switch between them. As in the case of younger children, they often do so as a function of whom they are talking to. In this video, a girl is fluently explaining a Lego plane she has made (the "24,000 model", as she calls it) in Spanish, English, and French.[25] You can hear adults ask her questions about the plane in each language in the same setting. The girl responds in the language each adult speaks. This switching behavior is typical. You can also hear switching in a triadic conversation: About five minutes into this video you can hear how, in a game with both his parents, 6-year-old Kevin speaks German with his mother but switches to Dutch when he addresses his father.[26]

The fact that many BFLA schoolchildren in bilingual homes do not speak the Non-Soc-L but only the Soc-L (Section 4.3) implies that they address Non-Soc-L-speaking parents in the Soc-L. As is the case for younger children, BFLA schoolchildren thus do not always use the same language that their parents speak to them. Section 4.5 discusses factors that may lie at the root of these language choice patterns.

Most (E)SLA children who hear only a Non-Soc-L from their parents at home likely speak it to them as well (Gathercole, 2007; the findings from De Houwer, 2007, imply this as well, see Section 4.3). However, most parents of 45 ESLA 5- to 6-year-olds with L1-Urdu reported that their children spoke mainly L2-Norwegian, the Soc-L, with friends and family (Karlsen et al., 2017). Parents and teachers of 139 BFLA and ESLA bilinguals reported that both at home and at school, children increasingly spoke more English (the Soc-L) than Spanish over the course of 5 school years (Oppenheim et al., 2020). Kaufman (2001) found that a third of 30 ESLA and SLA children between ages 6 and 13 spoke only L2-English to their Hebrew-speaking parents. The relative use of the Soc-L vs. the Non-Soc-L in conversations with peers was much higher in 8- to 10-year-old bilinguals than in younger bilingual schoolchildren (Jia et al., 2014). Fuller's (2012) ethnographic longitudinal study of L1-Spanish SLA students in the last three grades of a US transitional bilingual (Spanish–English) program showed how children started to use more and more L2-English rather than L1-Spanish with each other as time passed (see also Pease-Alvarez and Winsler, 1994). Bilingual students in Miami, Florida, almost exclusively spoke the Soc-L at school, even if they did not speak it well (Eilers et al., 2002). Children may use mixed utterances as well, but only in contexts where they feel comfortable using them. Spanish–English bilingual children used hardly any mixed utterances at school (Oller & Eilers, 2002).

---

[25] Piba18 [Screen name]. (2012, September 28). Trilingual Polyglot Little Girl Speaks Three Languages English French Spanish [Video]. *YouTube*. www.youtube.com/watch?v=3KswIJwGknA

[26] HaBilNet [Screen name]. (2017, September 26). Tweetalige kinderen [Video]. *YouTube*. www.youtube.com/watch?v=OdzA-9Gcpug

4.5 Factors Affecting Bilingual Development in Middle Childhood

As for BFLA and ESLA preschoolers, the length of time that BFLA and ESLA schoolchildren have heard each language may continue to affect their skills in each. Persici et al. (2019) compared 6.5- and 8.5-year-olds with bilingual input in German and Italian before age 3 (BFLA/very early ESLA) and demographically matched ESLA peers who had heard Italian from birth but started hearing L2-German at 3;6 or 4. Children's language learning histories affected language production and comprehension: Both groups performed at equal levels in Italian, but BFLA/very early ESLA children far outperformed ESLA children in L2-German. There were also differences in accuracy and speed in lexical judgment tasks in both languages (Section 4.1): Whereas BFLA and very early ESLA students performed similarly in both languages, ESLA students' performance was far better in their L1 than their L2.

Earlier exposure patterns also played a role in a longitudinal study of 228 (E) SLA children's Spanish and English skills at ages 6 and 8 (Collins & Toppelberg, 2021). Children had heard L1-Spanish from birth. Age of first regular exposure to L2-English started between ages 3 and 6. Children who had earlier attended ECEC (Early Childhood Education and Care) in Spanish had higher Spanish skills at ages 6 and 8 than those who had not. However, there was no association between attending Spanish ECEC and later L2-English skills, showing that maintaining the Non-Soc-L through ECEC is not a risk factor for developing the Soc-L. In fact, as in early childhood, knowledge of the L1 in (E)SLA can help develop L2 skills in middle childhood: The better ESLA schoolchildren's earlier narrative skills were in their L1, the better they were in their L2 a year later (Uccelli & Páez, 2007). Relatedly, Collier and Thomas' (2017) monumental study focusing on academic achievement in English showed that SLA schoolchildren in programs that used both their languages throughout the school years did much better than peers who were in English-only programs.

The longer children have heard a language, the more frequently they will have heard it. As in infancy and early childhood, frequency of input likely continues to play a role for bilingual children in middle childhood (Unsworth et al., 2014). Yet input frequency has hardly been featured in studies of bilingual schoolchildren. Compared to when children were not attending (pre)school, going to school in the Soc-L for about seven hours most workdays may increase the time of exposure to the Soc-L and may decrease the time that children hear the Non-Soc-L at home. How these changes affect the absolute amount of input in each language is largely unknown. Oppenheim et al. (2020) found that BFLA and ESLA schoolchildren's changing patterns of performance over the years, with them performing better in the Soc-L after they had performed better in the Non-Soc-L, corresponded with third-grade classrooms using much more of the Soc-L compared to the Non-Soc-L (earlier grades used both languages). Children also spoke much more of the Soc-L at home, mirroring results in Mancilla-Martinez and Lesaux (2011), who in addition reported much higher relative use of the Soc-L by mothers in speech to 11-year-olds compared to when their children were 4.5.

Language input at school is more diversified than that at home, is used in a variety of circumstances, and comes from many different speakers. The combined effect of these factors may help support the Soc-L. Gollan et al. (2015) found that also for the Non-Soc-L the number of speakers is important: The greater the number of people was who spoke the Non-Soc-L (Hebrew) with them, the better 22 Hebrew–English BFLA children aged between about 6 and 10 were on a Hebrew naming task. However, some children did not speak the Non-Soc-L.

Child-external factors relating to various aspects of the input as described so far may have different effects depending on what language is being assessed (Gutiérrez-Clellen & Kreiter, 2003). As outlined below, also child-internal factors may differentially relate to one particular language and not the other.

SLA children's motivation to learn a particular L2 may play a role in their developing proficiency (Haberzettl et al., 2013). Schoolchildren who know they will be moving to another country later in the school year likely want to invest less in the L2 than children who know they will be staying in the new country longer. Motivation may also have played a role in Homer's (Wagner-Gough, 1975) eagerness to engage with English L2 right from the start (Section 4.2). The fact that children typically learn to read and write mainly in the Soc-L likely strengthens their positive attitudes toward it.

Once SLA schoolchildren are able to speak two languages, even at rudimentary levels, they necessarily need to choose which one to use when. Children's language choices are not socially neutral. They may use each of their languages to mark social boundaries and indicate affiliation with some but not with others. Fuller (2012) documented how two SLA girls in the last years of a transitional bilingual program used L2-English with each other to set themselves apart from the other L1-Spanish children in their class. Attitudes and sensitivity to language hierarchies also played a role. Other L1-Spanish children in the classes that Fuller (2012) observed started to use more and more L2-English at school, likely because they realized that English carried far higher prestige: It was used exclusively in mainstream classrooms, and children aspired to transitioning to those mainstream classrooms. Also younger (E)SLA children may be sensitive to language hierarchies. Gibson et al. (2012) investigated the Spanish and English abilities of 124 5- to 7-year-olds with input to L1-Spanish in the home; 45% had started hearing L2-English at preschool (ESLA); 55% started hearing L2-English at school (SLA). Unsurprisingly, ESLA children had better L2 word comprehension and production abilities than SLA children. All children, however, showed a much wider gap between comprehension and production in L1-Spanish than in L2-English. Children were just not producing many words in the L1. Tests were carried out at school. Gibson et al. speculated that in the school environment, children were perhaps not keen on presenting themselves as Non-Soc-L speakers.

Positive attitudes toward the Soc-L may foster negative attitudes toward the Non-Soc-L, leading to common observations that children forbid parents to speak the Non-Soc-L when they are in earshot of classmates (review in De Houwer, 2020a). Negative attitudes toward the Non-Soc-L may be shaped by teachers' stances toward languages not used in school. Teachers may ignore children's Non-Soc-Ls, thus erasing part of their identities. Worse, teachers may explicitly express negative attitudes toward children's Non-Soc-Ls, for instance, by ridiculing or punishing children when they speak a Non-Soc-L at school (anecdotally documented throughout many Western societies). Through her in-depth ethnographic work relying on 300 hours of close observation of 5- to 6-year-old bilinguals in a Danish school, Karrebaek (2013) showed how children interiorized the monolingual, Danish-only ideology communicated by the staff, and socialized each other into just speaking Danish (the Soc-L) at school. If SLA children are bullied for not speaking the Soc-L well (as was the case in von Grünigen et al., 2012), they may soon realize that they need to focus on improving their Soc-L skills and not pay much attention to the Non-Soc-L.

Not speaking the Non-Soc-L in middle childhood is at least partly related to parental input patterns in the home. De Houwer (2007) surveyed families with at least one 6- to 9-year-old and at least one parent who spoke the Non-Soc-L at home. In 16% of 121 single-parent families, children did not speak the Non-Soc-L. Most were reared by a parent who spoke both the Soc-L and the Non-Soc-L. Non-Soc-L transmission in dual-parent families was even less successful: In 24% of 1,778 dual-parent families no child spoke the Non-Soc-L. There were large differences among families in proportions of children speaking the Non-Soc-L. These differences were a function of parental input patterns. ESLA children whose parents only spoke the Non-Soc-L usually also spoke it (97%; Section 4.3). Other, likely BFLA, children heard both languages at home, in bilingual families representing four parental input patterns: (i) Most frequently, both parents spoke the Non-Soc-L as well as the Soc-L. In 79% of these families, children spoke the Non-Soc-L. (ii) Next most frequent were families where both parents spoke the Soc-L and one parent also spoke the Non-Soc-L. These had the lowest chance (36%) of having children who spoke the Non-Soc-L. (iii) Next came families where both parents spoke the Non-Soc-L and one parent also spoke the Soc-L. These had the highest chance of having children who spoke the Non-Soc-L (93%). (iv) Least frequent were the so-called OPOL families (Section 2.1), where one parent spoke the Soc-L and the other parent the Non-Soc-L. Only in 74% of these did children speak the Non-Soc-L. In contrast to frequent claims to the contrary there was no parent gender effect for Non-Soc-L transmission: Male and female parents who spoke a Non-Soc-L had the same chance of having children who did so (see also Gathercole, 2007). The different parental input patterns in De Houwer (2007) may reflect differences in the absolute amount of Non-Soc-L input, combined with the possibility that in bilingual families with a parent who did not speak the Non-Soc-L at home, children identified with that parent rather than the other parent.

Parental discourse strategies encouraging children to use the Non-Soc-L in conversation remain important for bilingual schoolchildren (De Houwer & Nakamura, accepted for publication 2021; Yu, 2014). Longitudinal analyses of parent–child interaction in 68 US bilingual families showed that parents who used monolingual discourse strategies and consistently spoke either Cantonese or Mandarin (the Non-Soc-L) with their 6-year-olds had children who were still proficient in the Non-Soc-L at 7;6 (Park et al., 2012). In contrast, 6-year-olds whose parents used more bilingual discourse strategies with them, thus allowing the use of English, the Soc-L, in a conversation, had very low proficiency in the Non-Soc-L 1.5 years later, or had lost the ability to speak it. Parental use of discourse strategies and of the Non-Soc-L were dynamically related to children's proficiency. Parents of 6-year-olds who were less proficient in the Non-Soc-L used less support for the Non-Soc-L 1.5 years later, illustrating the many transactional processes taking place in parent–child interaction over time (Park et al., 2012).

Thus, as in early childhood, shifts in language choice patterns may lead to shifts in children's language proficiency. The combined effects of bilingual schoolchildren's often highly positive attitudes toward the Soc-L and their more frequent and more diversified learning experiences in it may lead to ever increasing proficiency in the Soc-L and to children's lesser use of the Non-Soc-L. Lesser use of the Non-Soc-L may lead to decreasing Non-Soc-L proficiency, even in SLA children. Yet, parental engagement with children that encourages continued Non-Soc-L use may be key in offsetting the overwhelming influence of the school language, leading to children who proudly speak both the Non-Soc-L and the Soc-L, as shown in this video featuring several bilingual children in the United States.[27]

4.6 Summary

We know very little about bilingual schoolchildren's abilities in the Non-Soc-L, and not enough about their abilities in the Soc-L. However, what evidence there is suggests that bilingual schoolchildren greatly expand their abilities in the Soc-L, regardless of whether they acquired the Soc-L from birth, as a preschooler, or after age 6. By the end of middle childhood, most bilingual children who first started regularly hearing the Soc-L before age 7 likely know the Soc-L better than the Non-Soc-L they acquired from birth. Bilingual schoolchildren generally appear to prefer speaking the Soc-L, and may have stopped speaking the Non-Soc-L by the end of middle childhood (or earlier), especially if they acquired the Soc-L from birth. As at earlier stages of development, factors likely supporting children's continued Non-Soc-L use are high frequency of language input and a continued communicative need to speak the Non-Soc-L as negotiated through parent–child interaction.

5 Socioeconomic Status and Bilingual Development in Childhood

Research on monolingual children has found low(er) socioeconomic status (SES) to be a risk factor for English language development in infancy (Burchinal et al., 2008), early childhood (Levine et al., 2020), and middle childhood (Linberg et al., 2019). Similarly, lower SES was correlated with lower linguistic abilities in studies of Italian (Dicataldo & Roch, 2020) and German (Linberg et al., 2019) monolinguals. In contrast, no relation between SES and Spanish monolingual infants lexical development has been found (DeAnda et al., 2016a; Jackson-Maldonado et al., 1993).

These contrasting findings for different languages complicate attempts at investigating the role of SES for bilingual children's development. A child could be showing SES influence on a linguistic measure in one language but not in the other. DeAnda et al. (2016a) investigated links between SES and 16-month-old bilingual infants' more frequently heard language. For 36 mostly Spanish-hearing infants there was no relation between maternal SES and vocabulary comprehension (see also Marchman et al., 2020). Yet for 25 mostly English-hearing infants there was, with higher-SES mothers having better performing infants. Although DeAnda et al. did not study the same children's

---

[27] Stephanie Meade. (2014, February 10). Many Languages, One America: The Voices of Our Children [Video]. *YouTube*. www.youtube.com/watch?v=1FToY3BfHRU

performance in two languages, these results suggest that bilingual children's development may differentially relate to the same SES factor depending on which language is assessed. This is exactly what Collins and Toppelberg (2021) found for 228 Spanish–English schoolchildren: English proficiency was related to SES, but Spanish proficiency was not, echoing findings for 90 Spanish–English BFLA toddlers (Place & Hoff, 2016). Similarly, Dutch–Turkish 6-year-olds' Turkish vocabulary was not related to SES, whereas Dutch vocabulary was (Prevoo et al., 2014). Furthermore, SES may correlate with measures combining both languages but not with single-language measures. Ramírez-Esparza et al. (2017) found this to be the case for Spanish–English 24-month-old BFLA infants' production vocabulary size. Also, SES differences may play out differently in bilingual vs. monolingual children (Korecky-Kröll et al., 2019).

If SES moderates child language development, it is through the ways in which parents interact with their children (shown for monolingual parents in Pace et al., 2017, and Scheele et al., 2010). In bilingual settings it may be particularly important to take into account maternal as well as paternal SES measures (Collins & Toppelberg, 2021; Prevoo et al., 2014; Scheele et al., 2010). Fathers may speak a different language to children than mothers, or may speak more of a particular language to children than mothers. However, the extent to which SES functions as the only or main factor underlying how parents verbally engage with children is not known. In bilingual families, where languages and hence cultures are in contact, culturally determined patterns of parent–child interaction may moderate or even clash with SES-related propensities toward particular interaction patterns (DeAnda et al., 2016a; Gampe et al., 2020; Ramírez-Esparza et al., 2017). SES and cultural interactions may help to explain findings such Byers-Heinlein et al.'s (2020) showing that 6- to 9-month-olds from higher-SES bilingual families preferred IDS more than peers from lower-SES bilingual families. However, the evidence was not very strong, and there was no SES difference for 12- to 15-month-olds (regardless of SES, all bilingual infants preferred IDS over ADS; Section 2.2).

In bilingual settings involving immigrant parents it is unclear which SES measures should be used (Gatt et al., 2020). Also, using just a single type of measure may not adequately capture SES: Income measures may miss highly educated parents who failed to monetize their social capital in the country to which they emigrated; measures focusing only on education may miss parents who are living in poverty in spite of being highly educated in their country of origin. There is the added difficulty that bilingual children's language learning histories and associated exposure patterns need to be taken into account. Dicataldo and Roch's (2020) study of a heterogeneous sample of 4- to 6-year-olds widely differing in both SES and degree of bilingual exposure demonstrated that, for some language measures, differences in SES were more relevant, regardless of bilingual experience, whereas other language measures were more correlated with degree of bilingual exposure but independent of SES.

Byers-Heinlein et al. (2019) convincingly argued that, because of the ubiquity of child bilingualism and relations between bilingualism and many aspects of development, developmental scientists should routinely document children's language backgrounds in any developmental research, including precise ages of first regular exposure to each language for bilinguals. They likewise proposed that scholars routinely report sample SES. These recommendations are also relevant to ethnographic work undertaken in sociolinguistically oriented research. Only with more extensive background documentation in studies of child bilinguals will the connections between individual children's language learning trajectories and the contexts in which they develop their bilingualism become clear.

6 Summary and Conclusion

6.1 Summary

There is a great deal of variability in children's developing bilingualism, and bilingual children form a very heterogeneous population in terms of the language-related developmental trajectories they take. Yet, in spite of the great number of different language pairs that children acquire, several generalizations can be made as a function of the three basic environmental settings in which children learn their languages: Bilingual First Language Acquisition (BFLA), Early Second Language Acquisition (ESLA), or SLA (Second Language Acquisition). These can be succinctly summarized:

1) Unlike in (E)SLA, BFLA children learn to understand two languages in early infancy.
2) Unlike in (E)SLA, BFLA children say words in two languages when they are 2 years old.
3) Unlike in (E)SLA, many BFLA children start to form short and then longer and more complex sentences in Language A and Language Alpha at virtually the same age. Typically, ESLA and SLA children first learn to say sentences in their L1. Only much later do sentences in the L2 appear.
4) BFLA preschoolers speak each language without any systematic morphosyntactic influence from the other language. This is not the case for ESLA preschoolers, nor for SLA schoolchildren, at least not in the first stages of non-imitated sentence production.

5) The mixed utterances that child bilinguals in early childhood may use mostly concern insertions of single words or phrases from language X into an utterance otherwise in language Y.

6) BFLA children hardly have an "accent" in their two languages. (E)SLA children frequently show influences from the L1 in the L2 at the sound level, especially when they first speak the L2. In many (E)SLA children, this "foreign accent" eventually disappears.

7) At school entry, the Soc-L is often the better developed language in BFLA children. For ESLA children the Non-Soc-L is usually better developed. SLA children only know their Non-Soc-L at the time of school entry.

8) Uneven development, where bilingual children of any age do not perform equally well in both languages, is common.

9) There is vast variability among (E)SLA schoolchildren in the degrees to which they develop proficiency in their Soc-L and in the rates of their Soc-L development.

10) By age 11, many bilingual children have high levels of proficiency in their Soc-L, even if they started learning it after age 6.

11) By age 11, many BFLA children have lost the ability to speak their Non-Soc-L. Many other bilingual children may have low levels of proficiency in their Non-Soc-L. BFLA and ESLA children appear at greatest risk.

12) Bilingual children can be highly proficient in two or more languages, regardless of when they started learning them.

13) By age 11 and often long before, bilingual schoolchildren who are able to form sentences in two languages can fluently switch from one language to the other in a single conversation.

14) Bilingual children of any age address others mainly in a language they know their interlocutors will understand.

Bilingual children's different language learning environments (BFLA, ESLA, and SLA) lead to a great heterogeneity of individual profiles for day-to-day language use across the first decade of life. It is important to recognize this heterogeneity both in clinical practice (De Houwer, 2018a) and in research. The fundamental differences between BFLA and ESLA in infancy and early childhood need to be taken into account much more than they are. Some studies incorrectly refer to toddlers who started hearing their L2 at 1 or 1;6 as BFLA children. Yet, early perception and word learning in BFLA infants' first 12 months is influenced by the presence of two input languages, as is early word production. This finding of different developmental paths warrants a clear distinction with ESLA infants who started off with monolingual input and added an L2 afterwards. By contrast, studies of preschoolers may refer to L1 and L2 even if children experienced no chronological difference between languages. This failure to distinguish between BFLA and ESLA preschoolers makes it impossible to correctly interpret any findings. If studies of bilingual schoolchildren do not give information on children's language learning trajectories, many results will be equally uninterpretable.

Developmentalists may be surprised not to see child gender featured so far. Child gender has hardly featured in studies of bilingual children focusing on language. Studies that have considered the possible role of gender have not found any relation with language outcomes (Groba et al., 2019; Kim et al., 2014; Lauro et al., 2020).

In Western societies, BFLA is often held up as the ideal way to become "truly" bilingual (many hundreds of students, parents, educators, and even researchers have expressed this idea to me over the years). Most people do not realize that many BFLA children do not, in fact, speak two languages after early childhood. ESLA and SLA children actually fare better, because by the end of middle childhood most are likely proficient in both the school language and the language heard at home. The idealization of BFLA may underlie the notion that it is best to start L2 learning as early in life as possible (hundreds of websites in various countries subscribe to this notion). Whereas there are no inherent reasons why children should not be given the chance to learn a new language from an early age, the strong belief in "the earlier, the better" is leading many parents to take up second jobs and loans in order to pay for (mostly English) foreign language classes, and sets up high expectations for children's rapid L2 learning. However, as reviewed in this Element, learning to proficiently speak two languages in childhood is not automatic: It takes a lot of time and practice. Supporting dual language learning also requires a great deal of effort on the part of people engaging with young children. The good news is that the *older* children are, the faster they are in learning a new language naturalistically. It takes 10-year-old BFLA children and monolinguals 10 years to learn to use a Soc-L at a 10-year-old level. SLA students develop Soc-L skills at a much faster pace: If they start acquiring the Soc-L at age 6, SLA students do not need 10 years to reach a 10-year-old level. Many will reach that level after 3 or 4 years. The main reasons for this later language learning advantage may lie in SLA children's greater cognitive maturity when they start learning their new L2, and in their greater prior experience with their first language.

All bilingual children in Soc-L education eventually learn to speak the Soc-L. The Non-Soc-L does not fare as well, and may be at risk of stagnating or being lost. As explained in Section 6.2, this has repercussions for families' harmonious bilingualism, that is, family members' subjectively neutral or positive experience with aspects of the bilingual setting they find themselves in (De Houwer, 2020a).

6.2 Harmonious Bilingualism

In a monolingual setting parents quite naturally expect children to speak the language they speak to them and to get better and better at speaking that language. Parents in a bilingual family will often have the same expectation. It comes as a shocking surprise to find that children do not speak the Non-Soc-L (De Houwer, 2017c). Parents may feel regret, remorse, and guilt. They also may feel anger at their children and may feel that children reject them by rejecting their language, thus detracting from parental well-being, and, thus, harmonious bilingualism (reviews in De Houwer, 2017c, 2020a). Children who speak only the Soc-L may feel embarrassed that they can no longer communicate with monolingual Non-Soc-L-speaking grandparents. As young adults, they may feel that their parents did not do enough to support their development in the Non-Soc-L and may deeply regret not speaking the Non-Soc-L (Nakamura, 2020). Language choices in the family strongly influence family dynamics and interpersonal relationships among family members (Müller et al., 2020).

   Bilingual children need not only develop skills in the Non-Soc-L. They need to develop two languages. If they do so, their well-being is enhanced (De Houwer, 2020a). Bilinguals in early and middle childhood with better skills in each language than peers had better social-emotional skills (Sun et al., 2021). However, on the way toward developing their languages children encounter several hurdles that negatively impact their well-being, and thus harmonious bilingualism. The clearest sign that children may feel unhappy in relation to their linguistic environment comes from monolingual preschoolers who find themselves in a group setting where a language is used that they do not understand. As described in Section 3.2.1, many ESLA-to-be children withdraw from the communicative goings-on in that group setting, may show signs of depression, and are silent. At home they may also appear depressed, but they are still speaking their L1 (Drury, 2007). Manigand (1999) described how he observed several silent preschoolers in L2-preschools and tried to interpret the nature of their silence, taking into account information about children's home and cultural backgrounds. With much patience he then tried to engage these children in one-on-one interaction, at first nonverbally; however, without much success, until he said a few words in the children's Non-Soc-L, leading to smiles and diminished reluctance to interact with him (see also Chang et al., 2007). Eventually, through Manigand translating words between the Non-Soc-L and the Soc-L and with the help of pictures and games, children started to say some words in the Soc-L. Itoh and Hatch (1978) recounted a similar trajectory. SLA schoolchildren may experience lower levels of self-control and interpersonal skills and higher levels of internalizing problems compared to bilingual children who speak the Soc-L at school entry (Han, 2010; Han & Huang, 2010). To avoid such ill effects of a relatively late start in the Soc-L, Han (2010) proposed that schools should implement high-quality L2 programs (Kim et al., 2015), rather than the "sink-or-swim" approach characteristic of so many schools.

Children and families need positive support. Childcare centers and pre-schools should ensure that ESLA preschoolers do not experience a possibly traumatic long "silent period." Pedagogical approaches that recognize and value all languages that children bring to preschool are essential (Chilla & Niebuhr-Siebert, 2017; Chumak-Horbatsch, 2012). With reference to Spanish–English US families, Hoff and Ribot (2017, p. 245) wrote: "Just as pediatricians encourage English-speaking parents to read books and use rich turn-taking conversations with their monolingual children, they should offer the same powerful advice to parents speaking Spanish with their bilingual children." Initiatives like the Háblame Bebé[28] app developed by Baralt et al. (2020) and the research-based Harmonious Bilingualism Network[29] may help families to guide their children on a constructive and positive bilingual path.

6.3 Parting Words

Research on bilingual children has grown exponentially in the last two and a half decades (Bayram et al., 2018). New research on bilingual children is published in widely different publication channels, reflecting the diversity of the disciplines and subdisciplines in which bilingual children's language development and its supporting factors are investigated: developmental psycholinguistics, sociolinguistics, cognitive and developmental psychology, education, applied linguistics, sociology, neuropsychology, social work, psychopathology, clinical linguistics, and more. These fields differ widely in their methods and orientations. Given this diversity and the extraordinary wealth of information available, this Element has necessarily had to be selective. Furthermore, statements indicating lack of knowledge about a particular phenomenon may be in error, either because I was unaware of the relevant research or because a new publication has appeared since this Element was written.

However, in spite of the wealth of studies available, bilingual children's individual trajectories beyond the first 3.5 years of life have hardly been documented. This means there is little information on the developmental course of bilingual children's language comprehension and production beyond the middle of early childhood. Studies tend to focus on language outcomes for groups of children, often averaging findings. This obscures individual developmental paths.

---

[28] Háblame Bebé (2018) [website]. https://hablamebebe.org/
[29] HaBilNet (n.d.) [website] www.habilnet.org/

Even though many studies have explored factors influencing bilingual outcomes at one or more points in development, "almost nothing is known about the long-term impact of home language management on children's . . . bilingual development" (Schwartz, 2020). There is an urgent need for developmental studies to trace the dynamics of family language choices and practices over the years and to determine how families manage the challenges associated with living in environments that do not necessarily support children's bilingualism.

The surge in research interest in bilingual children has undoubtedly been helped by the general realization that bilingual children account for a very large and ever increasing proportion of the children in preschools and schools across the globe (Section 1). This increase has gone hand in hand with highly increased mobility worldwide. Although there have been severe restrictions on international mobility in relation to the SARS-CoV-2 virus, child bilingualism will continue to be part and parcel of societies across the globe. It is my hope that scholars everywhere will continue to give child bilingualism the attention it inherently deserves, without the still all-too-frequent focus on comparisons with monolinguals, and notions of "accelerated" or "delayed" development in bilinguals. A deep-seated monolingual bias in many Western societies is one reason that bilingual children may fail to experience harmonious bilingual development. The research community needs to support harmonious bilingualism by investigating it with attention to the many factors that threaten or foster it. Only increased knowledge of these factors will help us to truly understand bilingual development.

References

Aarssen, J. (1996). *Relating events in two languages: Acquisition of cohesive devices by Turkish-Dutch bilingual children at school age.* Tilburg: Tilburg University Press.

Águila, E., Ramon-Casas, M., Pons, F., & Bosch, L. (2007). La medida del léxico productivo inicial: Aplicación de un cuestionario para la población bilingüe. In E. Diez-Itza (Ed.), *Estudios de desarrollo del lenguaje y educación* (Vol. 32). Oviedo, Spain: ICE Monografias de Aula Abierta, 163–71.

Ahrenholz, B., Hövelbrinks, B., Maak, D., & Zippel, W. (2013). Mehrsprachigkeit an Thüringer Schulen (MaTS) – Ergebnisse einer Fragebogenerhebung zu Mehrsprachigkeit an Erfurter Schulen. In İ. Dirim & I. Oomen-Welke (Eds.), *Mehrsprachigkeit in der Klasse: Wahrnehmen – Aufgreifen – Fördern.* Stuttgart: Fillibach bei Klett, 43–58.

Andruski, J. E., Casielles, E., & Nathan, G. (2014). Is bilingual babbling language-specific? Some evidence from a case study of Spanish-English dual acquisition. *Bilingualism: Language and Cognition, 17*, 660–72. doi: http://doi.org/10.1017/S1366728913000655

Argyri, E., & Sorace, A. (2007). Crosslinguistic influence and language dominance in older bilingual children. *Bilingualism: Language and Cognition, 10*, 79–99. doi:http://doi.org/10.1017/S1366728906002835

Armon-Lotem, S., & Meir, N. (2019). The nature of exposure and input in early bilingualism. In A. De Houwer & L. Ortega (Eds.), *The Cambridge handbook of bilingualism.* Cambridge: Cambridge University Press, 193–212. doi: http://doi.org/10.1017/9781316831922.011

Autorengruppe Bildungsberichterstattung. (2018). *Bildung in Deutschland 2018. Ein indikatorengestützter Bericht mit einer Analyse zu Wirkungen und Erträgen von Bildung.* Bielefeld: wby Media. doi:http://doi.org/10.3278/6001820fw

Babatsouli, E., & Ball, M. J. (Eds.) (2020). *An anthology of bilingual child phonology.* Bristol: Multilingual Matters. doi:http://doi.org/10.21832/9781788928427

Baralt, M., Darcy-Mahoney, A., & Brito, N. H. (2020). Háblame Bebé: A phone application intervention to support Hispanic children's early language environments and bilingualism. *Child Language Teaching & Therapy, 36* (1), 33–57. doi:http://doi.org/10.1177/0265659020903779

Bayram, F., Miller, D., Rothman, J., & Serratrice, L. (2018). Studies in bilingualism: 25 years in the making. In D. Miller, F. Bayram, J. Rothman, &

L. Serratrice (Eds.), *Bilingual cognition and language: The state of the science across its subfields.* Amsterdam: John Benjamins, 1–12. doi:http://doi.org/10.1075/sibil.54.01bay

Bergelson, E., & Swingley, D. (2012). At 6–9 months, human infants know the meanings of many common nouns. *PNAS, 109*(9), 3253–3258. doi:http://doi.org/10.1073/pnas.1113380109

Bhatia, T. K., & Ritchie, W. C. (2013). *The handbook of bilingualism and multilingualism* (2nd ed.). Oxford: Blackwell. doi:http://doi.org/10.1002/9781118332382

Bialystok, E., Luk, G., Peets, K., & Yang, S. (2010). Receptive vocabulary differences in monolingual and bilingual children. *Bilingualism: Language and Cognition, 13*, 525–31. doi:http://doi.org/10.1017/S1366728909990423

Bijeljac-Babic, R., Höhle, B., & Nazzi, T. (2016). Early prosodic acquisition in bilingual infants: The case of the perceptual trochaic bias. *Frontiers in Psychology, 7*, 210. doi:http://doi.org/10.3389/fpsyg.2016.00210

Blom, E. (2010). Effects of input on the early grammatical development of bilingual children. *International Journal of Bilingualism, 14*(4), 422–446. doi:http://doi.org/10.1177/1367006910370917

Blom, E., & Paradis, J. (2015). Sources of individual differences in the acquisition of tense inflection by English second language learners with and without specific language impairment. *Applied Psycholinguistics*, 36, 953–976. doi: http://doi.org/10.1017/S014271641300057X

Bornstein, M. H. (2009). Toward a model of culture↔parent↔child transactions. In A. Sameroff (Ed.), *The transactional model of development: How children and contexts shape each other.* Washington, DC: American Psychological Association, 139–161. doi:http://doi.org/10.1037/11877-008

Bornstein, M. H. (2019). A developmentalist's viewpoint: "It's about time!" Ecological systems, transaction, and specificity as key developmental principles in children's changing worlds. In R. D. Parke & G. H. Elder, Jr. (Eds.), *Children in changing worlds. Sociocultural and temporal perspectives.* Cambridge: Cambridge University Press, 277–286. doi:http://doi.org/10.1017/9781108264846.010

Bornstein, M. H. & Haynes, O. M. (1998). Vocabulary competence in early childhood: Measurement, latent construct, and predictive validity. *Child Development, 69*(3), 654–671. doi:http://doi.org/10.1111/j.1467-8624.1998.tb06235.x

Bosch, L., Figueras, F., Teixidó, M., & Ramon-Casas, M. (2013). Rapid gains in segmenting fluent speech when words match the rhythmic unit: Evidence from infants acquiring syllable-timed languages. *Frontiers in Psychology, 4*, 106. doi:http://doi.org/10.3389/fpsyg.2013.00106

Bosch, L., & Ramon-Casas, M. (2011). Variability in vowel production by bilingual speakers: Can input properties hinder the early stabilization of contrastive categories? *Journal of Phonetics*, 39, 514–526. doi:http://doi.org/10.1016/j.wocn.2011.02.001

Brojde, C. L., Ahmed, S., & Colunga, E. (2012). Bilingual and monolingual children attend to different cues when learning new words. *Frontiers in Psychology*, *3*, 155. doi:http://doi.org/10.3389/fpsyg.2012.00155

Budde-Spengler, N., Sachse, S., & Rinker, T. (2018). The relationship between input factors and early lexical knowledge in Turkish–German children. *International Journal of Bilingual Education and Bilingualism*. doi:http://doi.org/10.1080/13670050.2018.1543647

Burchinal, M., Vernon-Feagans, L., & Cox, M. (2008). Cumulative social risk, parenting, and infant development in rural low-income communities. *Parenting: Science and Practice*, *8*, 41–69. doi:http://doi.org/10.1080/15295190701830672

Burns, T., Yoshida, K., Hill, K., & Werker, J. T. (2007). The development of phonetic representation in bilingual and monolingual infants. *Applied Psycholinguistics*, *28*, 455–474. doi:http://doi.org/10.1017/S0142716407070257

Byers-Heinlein, K. (2017). Bilingualism affects 9-month-old infants' expectations about how words refer to kinds. *Developmental Science*, *20*, e12486. doi:http://doi.org/10.1111/desc.12486

Byers-Heinlein, K., Tsui, A., Bergmann, C., Black, A. K., Brown, A., Carbajal, M. J., … Wermelinger, S. (2021). A multi-lab study of bilingual infants: Exploring the preference for infant-directed speech. *Advances in Methods and Practices in Psychological Science, 4*(1), 1–30 [Registered report]. doi:https://doi.org/10.1177/2515245920974622

Byers-Heinlein, K., Burns, T. C., & Werker, J. F. (2010). The roots of bilingualism in newborns. *Psychological Science*, *21*(3), 343–348. doi:http://doi.org/10.1177/0956797609360758

Byers-Heinlein, K., Esposito, A. G., Winsler, A., Marian, V., Castro, D. C., & Luk, G. (2019). The case for measuring and reporting bilingualism in developmental research. *Collabra: Psychology*, *5*(1), 37. doi:http://doi.org/10.1525/collabra.233

Cantone, K. F. (2007). *Code-switching in bilingual children*. Dordrecht, the Netherlands: Springer. doi:http://doi.org/10.1007/978-1-4020-5784-7

Carbajal, M. J., & Peperkamp, S. (2020). Dual language input and the impact of language separation on early lexical development. *Infancy*, *25*(1), 22–45. doi:http://doi.org/10.1111/infa.12315

Chang, F., Crawford, G., Early, D., Bryant, D., Howes, C., Burchinal, M., Barbarin, O., Clifford, R., & Pianta, R. (2007). Spanish-speaking children's social and language development in pre-kindergarten classrooms. *Early Education and Development, 18*(2), 243–69. doi:http://doi.org/10.1080/10409280701282959

Chevalier, S. (2015). *Trilingual language acquisition: Contextual factors influencing active trilingualism in early childhood.* Amsterdam: John Benjamins. doi:http://doi.org/10.1075/tilar.16

Chevrot, J.-P., & Ghimenton, A. (2019). Bilingualism and bidialectalism. In A. De Houwer & L. Ortega (Eds.), *The Cambridge handbook of bilingualism.* Cambridge: Cambridge University Press, 510–23. doi:http://doi.org/10.1017/9781316831922.026

Chilla, S., & Niebuhr-Siebert, S. (2017). *Mehrsprachigkeit in der KiTa. Grundlagen – Konzepte – Bildung.* Stuttgart: Kohlhammer.

Chondrogianni, V., & Marinis, T. (2011). Differential effects of internal and external factors on the development of vocabulary, morphology and complex syntax in successive bilingual children. *Linguistic Approaches to Bilingualism, 1,* 223–248. doi:http://doi.org/10.1075/lab.1.3.05cho

Chondrogianni V, & Schwartz, R. G. (2020). Case and word order in Greek heritage children. *Journal of Child Language, 47,* 766–795. doi:http://doi.org/10.1017/S0305000919000849

Chumak-Horbatsch, R. (2012). *Linguistically Appropriate Practice: A guide for working with young immigrant children.* Toronto: University of Toronto Press.

Clark, E. V. (1993). *The lexicon in acquisition.* Cambridge: Cambridge University Press. doi:http://doi.org/10.1017/CBO9780511554377

Clark, E. V. (2003). Critical periods, time, and practice. *University of Pennsylvania Working Papers in Linguistics, 9*(2), 39–48.

Collier, V., & Thomas, W. P. (2017). Validating the power of bilingual schooling: Thirty-two years of large-scale, longitudinal research. *Annual Review of Applied Linguistics, 37,* 203–17. doi:http://doi.org/10.1017/S0267190517000034

Collins, B., & Toppelberg, C. (2021). The role of socioeconomic and sociocultural predictors of Spanish and English proficiencies of young Latino children of immigrants. *Journal of Child Language, 48*(1), 129–156. doi:http://doi.org/10.1017/S0305000920000203

Comeau, L., & Genesee, F. (2001). Bilingual children's repair strategies during dyadic communication. In J. Cenoz & F. Genesee (Eds.), *Trends in bilingual acquisition.* Amsterdam: John Benjamins, 231–256. doi:http://doi.org/10.1075/tilar.1.11com

Conboy, B. T., & Thal, D. (2006). Ties between the lexicon and grammar: Cross-sectional and longitudinal studies of bilingual toddlers. *Child Development*, 77, 712–735. doi:http://doi.org/10.1111/j.1467-8624.2006.00899.x

Cote, L. R., & Bornstein, M. H. (2014). Productive vocabulary among three groups of bilingual American children: Comparison and prediction. *First Language*, *34*, 467–485. doi:http://doi.org/10.1177/0142723714560178

Cruz-Ferreira, M. (2006). *Three is a crowd? Acquiring Portuguese in a trilingual environment*. Clevedon: Multilingual Matters. doi:http://doi.org /10.21832/9781853598395

Czinglar, C., Rüdiger, J. O., Korecky-Kröll, K., Uzunkaya-Sharma, K., & Dressler, W. U. (2017). Inputfaktoren im DaZ-Erwerb von sukzessiv bilin-gualen Kindern mit L1 Türkisch. In I. Fuchs, S. Jeuk, & W. Knapp (Eds.), *Mehrsprachigkeit: Spracherwerb, Unterrichtsprozesse, Seiteneinstieg: Beiträge aus dem 11. Workshop "Kinder und Jugendliche mit Migrationshintergrund."* Stuttgart: Fillibach bei Klett, 15–34.

Dahoun, Z. K. S. (1995). *Les couleurs du silence. Le mutisme des enfants de migrants*. Paris: Calmann-Lévy.

David, A., & Li, W. (2008). Individual differences in the lexical development of French–English bilingual children. *International Journal of Bilingualism and Bilingual Education*, *11*(5), 598–618. doi:http://doi.org/10.1080 /13670050802149200

Davidson, D., Jergovic, D., Imami, Z., & Theodos, V. (1997). Monolingual and bilingual children's use of the mutual exclusivity constraint. *Journal of Child Language*, *24*, 3–24. doi:http://doi.org/10.1017/S0305000996002917

DeAnda, S., Arias-Trejo, N., Poulin-Dubois, D., Zesiger, P., & Friend, M. (2016a). Minimal second language exposure, SES, and early word comprehen-sion: New evidence from a direct assessment. *Bilingualism: Language and Cognition*, *19*(1), 162–180. doi:http://doi.org/10.1017/S1366728914000820

DeAnda, S., Poulin-Dubois, D., Zesiger, P., & Friend, M. (2016b). Lexical processing and organization in bilingual first language acquisition: Guiding future research. *Psychological Bulletin*, *142*, 655–667. doi:http://doi.org/10 .1037/bul0000042

De Houwer, A. (1990). *The acquisition of two languages from birth: A case study*. Cambridge: Cambridge University Press. doi:https://doi.org/10.1017 /CBO9780511519789

De Houwer, A. (2003). Home languages spoken in officially monolingual Flanders: A survey. *Plurilingua*, *24*, 79–96.

De Houwer, A. (2007). Parental language input patterns and children's bilingual use. *Applied Psycholinguistics*, *28*(3), 411–424. doi:http://doi.org/10.1017 /S0142716407070221

De Houwer, A. (2009). *Bilingual First Language Acquisition.* Bristol: Multilingual Matters. doi:http://doi.org/10.21832/9781847691507

De Houwer, A. (2014). The absolute frequency of maternal input to bilingual and monolingual children: A first comparison. In T. Grüter & J. Paradis (Eds.), *Input and experience in bilingual development.* Amsterdam: John Benjamins, 37–58. doi:http://doi.org/10.1075/tilar.13.03deh

De Houwer, A. (2015a). Early foreign language teaching: Some critical remarks and some recommendations. *Babylonia,* 01(14), 14–21.

De Houwer, A. (2015b). Integration und Interkulturalität in Kindertagesstätten und in Kindergärten: Die Rolle der Nichtumgebungssprache für das Wohlbefinden von Kleinkindern. In E. Reichert-Garschhammer, C. Kieferle, M. Wertfein, & F. Becker-Stoll (Eds.), *Inklusion und Partizipation. Vielfalt als Chance und Anspruch.* Göttingen: Vandenhoeck & Ruprecht, 113–125.

De Houwer, A. (2017a). Bilingual language input environments, intake, maturity and practice. *Bilingualism: Language and Cognition,* 20, 19–20. doi: http://doi.org/10.1017/S1366728916000298

De Houwer, A. (2017b). Early multilingualism and language awareness. In J. Cenoz, D. Gorter & S. May (Eds.), *Language awareness and multilingualism. Encyclopedia of language and education* (3rd ed.). Cham: Springer, 83–97. doi:http://doi.org/10.1007/978-3-319-02240-6_6

De Houwer, A. (2017c). Minority language parenting in Europe and children's well-being. In N. Cabrera & B. Leyendecker (Eds.), *Handbook on positive development of minority children and youth.* Cham: Springer, 231–246. doi: http://doi.org/10.1007/978-3-319-43645-6_14

De Houwer, A. (2018a). Input, context and early child bilingualism: Implications for clinical practice. In A. Bar-On & Dorit Ravid (Eds.), *Handbook of communication disorders: Theoretical, empirical, and applied linguistic perspectives.* Berlin: Walter de Gruyter, 599–616. doi:http://doi.org/10.1515/9781614514909-030

De Houwer, A. (2018b). The role of language input environments for language outcomes and language acquisition in young bilingual children. In D. Miller, F. Bayram, J. Rothman, & L. Serratrice (Eds.), *Bilingual cognition and language: The state of the science across its subfields.* Amsterdam: John Benjamins, 127–153. doi:http://doi.org/10.1075/sibil.54.07hou

De Houwer, A. (2019a). Equitable evaluation of bilingual children's's language knowledge using the CDI: It really matters who you ask. *Journal of Monolingual and Bilingual Speech,* 1(1), 32–54. doi:http://doi.org/10.1558/jmbs.11184

De Houwer, A. (2019b). Language choice in bilingual interaction. In A. De Houwer & L. Ortega (Eds.), *The Cambridge Handbook of Bilingualism.*

Cambridge: Cambridge University Press, 324–348. doi:http://doi.org/10 .1017/9781316831922.018

De Houwer, A. (2019c). Uninstructed language acquisition in multiple language learners. In J. Darquennes, J. Salmons, & W. Vandenbussche (Eds.), *Language contact: An international handbook.* Berlin: Mouton de Gruyter, 183–196. doi:http://doi.org/10.1515/9783110435351-016

De Houwer, A. (2020a). Harmonious Bilingualism: Well-being for families in bilingual settings. In S. Eisenchlas & A. Schalley (Eds.), *Handbook of home language maintenance and development. Social and affective factors.* Berlin: Mouton de Gruyter, 63–83. doi:http://doi.org/10.1515/9781501510175-004

De Houwer, A. (2020b). Why do so many children who hear two languages speak just a single language? *Zeitschrift für Interkulturellen Fremdsprachenunterricht, 25*(1), 7–26.

De Houwer, A., & Bornstein, M. H. (2016a). Balance patterns in early bilingual acquisition: A longitudinal study of word comprehension and production. In C. Silva-Corvalán & J. Treffers-Daller (Eds.), *Language dominance in bilinguals. Issues of measurement and operationalization.* Cambridge: Cambridge University Press, 134–155. doi:http://doi.org/10.1017/CBO9781107375345.007

De Houwer, A., & Bornstein, M. H. (2016b). Bilingual mothers' language choice in child-directed speech: Continuity and change. *Journal of Multilingual and Multicultural Development, 37*(7), 680–693. doi:http://doi .org/10.1080/01434632.2015.1127929

De Houwer, A., Bornstein, M. H., & De Coster, S. (2006). Early understanding of two words for the same thing: A CDI study of lexical comprehension in infant bilinguals. *International Journal of Bilingualism, 10,* 331–347. doi: http://doi.org/10.1177/13670069060100030401

De Houwer, A., Bornstein, M. H., & Putnick, D. L. (2014). A bilingual-monolingual comparison of young children's vocabulary size: Evidence from comprehension and production. *Applied Psycholinguistics, 35,* 1189–1211. doi:http://doi.org/10.1017/S0142716412000744

De Houwer, A., & Nakamura, J. (accepted for publication 2021). Developmental perspectives on parents' use of discourse strategies with bilingual children. Routledge.

De Houwer, A., & Ortega, L. (2019). Introduction: Learning, using, and unlearning more than one language. In A. De Houwer & L. Ortega (Eds.), *The Cambridge handbook of bilingualism.* Cambridge: Cambridge University Press, 1–12. doi:http://doi.org/10.1017/9781316831922.001

Dicataldo, R., & Roch, M. (2020). Are the effects of variation in quantity of daily bilingual exposure and socioeconomic status on language and cognitive abilities independent in preschool children? *International Journal of*

Environmental Research and Public Health, 17, 4570. doi:http://doi.org/10
.3390/ijerph17124570

Drury, R. (2007). *Young bilingual learners at home and school: Researching multilingual voices*. Stoke on Trent: Trentham Books.

Dubiel, B., & Guilfoyle, E. (2017). Language strength in bilingual children: The Child HALA test. *Heritage Language Journal, 14*(1), 1–29.

Dunn, L. M., & Dunn, L. M. (1997). *Peabody Picture Vocabulary Test* (3rd ed.). Minneapolis, MN: Pearson Assessments.

Durrant, S., Delle Luche, C., Cattani, A., & Floccia, C. (2014). Monodialectal and multidialectal infants' representation of familiar words. *Journal of Child Language, 42*, 447–465. doi:http://doi.org/10.1017/S0305000914000063

Eilers, R. E., Oller, D. K., & Cobo-Lewis, A. B. (2002). Bilingualism and cultural assimilation in Miami Hispanic children. In D. K. Oller & R. E. Eilers (Eds.), *Language and literacy in bilingual children*. Clevedon: Multilingual Matters, 43–63.

Eilers, R. E., Pearson, B. Z., & Cobo-Lewis, A. B. (2006). Social factors in bilingual development: The Miami experience. In P. McCardle & E. Hoff (Eds.), *Childhood bilingualism: Research on infancy through school age*. Clevedon: Multilingual Matters, 68–90.

Ertanir, B., Kratzmann, J., Frank, M., Jahreiss, S., & Sachse, S. (2018). Dual language competencies of Turkish–German children growing up in Germany: Factors supportive of functioning dual language development. *Frontiers in Psychology, 9*(2261). doi:http://doi.org/10.3389/fpsyg.2018.02261

Ertanir, B., Kratzmann, J., & Sachse, S. (2019). Sozio-emotionale Kompetenzen mehrsprachiger Kindergartenkinder und deren Wechselwirkungen mit den Sprachleistungen im Deutschen. *Zeitschrift für Entwicklungspsychologie und Pädagogische Psychologie, 51*(1), 31–44. doi:http://doi.org/10.1026/0049-8637/a000207

Fennell, C. T., & Byers-Heinlein, K. (2014). You sound like Mommy: Bilingual and monolingual infants learn words best from speakers typical of their language environments. *International Journal of Behavioral Development, 38*, 309–316. doi:http://doi.org/10.1026/0049-8637/a00020710.1177/0165025414530631

Fenson, L., Dale, P., Reznick, J. S., Thal, D., Bates, E., Hartung, J., Pethick, S. J., & Reilly, J. (1993). *MacArthur Communicative Development Inventories: User's guide and technical manual*. San Diego, CA: Singular Publishing Group.

Fish, M. S., García-Sierra, A., Ramírez-Esparza, N., & Kuhl, P. K. (2017). Infant-directed speech in English and Spanish: Assessments of monolingual and bilingual caregiver VOT. *Journal of Phonetics, 63*, 19–34. doi: https://doi.org/10.1016/j.wocn.2017.04.003

Fuller, J. M. (2012). *Bilingual pre-teens: Competing ideologies and multiple identities in the U.S. and Germany.* New York, NY: Routledge. doi:http://doi .org/10.4324/9780203110645

Fuller, J. M. (2019). Ideologies of language, bilingualism, and monolingualism. In A. De Houwer & L. Ortega (Eds.), *The Cambridge handbook of bilingualism.* Cambridge: Cambridge University Press, 119–134. doi:http://doi.org/10 .1017/9781316831922.007

Gagarina, N., & Klassert, A. (2018). Input dominance and development of home language in Russian-German bilinguals. *Frontiers in Communication*, 3(40). doi:http://doi.org/10.3389/fcomm.2018.00040

Gampe, A., Hartmann, L., & Daum, M. M. (2020). Dynamic interaction patterns of monolingual and bilingual infants with their parents. *Journal of Child Language*, 47(1), 45–63. doi:http://doi.org/10.1017 /S0305000919000631

Gampe, A., Wermelinger, S., & Daum, M. M. (2019). Bilingual children adapt to the needs of their communication partners, monolinguals do not. *Child Development*, 90(1), 98–107. doi:http://doi.org/10.1111/cdev.13190

Garcia-Sierra, A., Rivera-Gaxiola, M., Percaccio, C. R., Conboy, B. T., Romo, H., Klarman, L., & Kuhl, P. K. (2011). Bilingual language learning: An ERP study relating early brain responses to speech, language input, and later word production. *Journal of Phonetics*, 39(4), 546–557. doi:http://doi .org/10.1016/j.wocn.2011.07.002

Gathercole, V. C. M. (Ed.) (2007). *Language transmission in bilingual families in Wales.* Cardiff: Welsh Language Board.

Gathercole, V. C. M., & Thomas, E. M. (2009). Bilingual first-language development: Dominant language takeover, threatened minority language take-up. *Bilingualism: Language and Cognition*, 12, 213–237. doi:http://doi.org/10 .1017/S1366728909004015

Gatt, D., Baldacchino, R., & Dodd, B. (2020). Which measure of socioeconomic status best predicts bilingual lexical abilities and how? A focus on four-year-olds exposed to two majority languages. *Journal of Child Language*, 47(4), 737–765. doi:http://doi.org/10.1017/S0305000919000886

Genesee, F., Boivin, I., & Nicoladis, E. (1996). Talking with strangers: A study of bilingual children's communicative competence. *Applied Psycholinguistics*, 17, 427–442. doi:http://doi.org/10.1017/S0142716400008183

Genesee, F., & Delcenserie, A. (Eds.) (2016). *Starting over – The language development in internationally-adopted children.* Amsterdam: John Benjamins. doi:http://doi.org/10.1075/tilar.18

Gibson, T. A., Oller, D. K., Jarmulowicz, L., & Ethington, C. A. (2012). The receptive-expressive gap in the vocabulary of young second-language learners: Robustness and possible mechanisms. *Bilingualism: Language and Cognition, 15*, 102–116. doi:http://doi.org/10.1017/S1366728910000490

Gollan, T. H., Starr, J., & Ferreira, V. S. (2015). More than use it or lose it: The number-of-speakers effect on heritage language proficiency. *Psychonomic Bulletin and Review, 22*(1), 147–55. doi:http://doi.org/10.3758/s13423-014-0649-7

Granfeldt, J., Schlyter, J., & Kihlstedt, M. (2007). French as cL2, 2L1 and L1 in pre-school children. In J. Granfeldt (Ed.), *Studies in Romance bilingual acquisition – age of onset and development of French and Spanish*. Lund: Lund University, 7–42.

Groba, A., De Houwer, A., Obrig, H., & Rossi, S. (2019). Bilingual and monolingual first language acquisition experience differentially shapes children's property term learning: Evidence from behavioral and neurophysiological measures. *Brain Sciences, 9*(2), 40. doi:http://doi.org/10.3390/brainsci9020040

Grosjean, F. (1989). Neurolinguists beware! The bilingual is not two monolinguals in one person. *Brain and Language, 36*, 3–15. doi:http://doi.org/10.1016/0093-934X(89)90048-5

Grosjean, F., & Byers-Heinlein, K. (2018). *The listening bilingual: Speech perception, comprehension, and bilingualism*. Hoboken, NJ: John Wiley & Sons. doi:http://doi.org/10.1002/9781118835722

Gutiérrez-Clellen, V. F., & Kreiter, J. (2003). Understanding child bilingual acquisition using parent and teacher reports. *Applied Psycholinguistics, 24*, 267–288. doi:http://doi.org/10.1017/S0142716403000158

Haberzettl, S., Dimroth, C., Wulff, N., & Czinglar, C. (2013). Erwerb des Deutschen als Zweitsprache im Grundschulalter. In A. Berndt (Ed.), *Fremdsprachen in der Perspektive lebenslangen Lernens*. Frankfurt am Main: Peter Lang, 143–161.

Haman, E., Łuniewska, M., & Pomiechowska, B. (2015). Designing Cross-Linguistic Lexical Tasks (CLTs) for bilingual preschool children. In S. Armon-Lotem, J. de Jong, & M. Meir (Eds.), *Methods for assessing multilingual children: Disentangling bilingualism from language impairment*. Bristol: Multilingual Matters, 194–238. doi:http://doi.org/10.21832/9781783093137-010

Hammer, C. S., Komaroff, E., Rodriguez, B. L., Lopez, L. M., Scarpino, S. E., & Goldstein, B. (2012). Predicting Spanish-English bilingual children's language abilities. *Journal of Speech, Language, and Hearing Research, 55* (5), 1251–1264. doi:http://doi.org/10.1044/1092-4388(2012/11-0016)

Han, W.-J. (2010). Bilingualism and socioemotional well-being. *Children and Youth Services Review, 32*, 720–31. doi:http://doi.org/10.1016/j.childyouth.2010.01.009

Han, W.-J., & Huang, C.-C. (2010). The forgotten treasure: Bilingualism and Asian children's emotional and behavioral health. *American Journal of Public Health, 100*(5), 831–838. doi:http://doi.org/10.2105/AJPH.2009.174219

Hatch, E. M. (Ed.) (1978). *Second language acquisition: A book of readings*. Rowley, MA: Newbury House Publishers.

Havy, M., Bouchon, C., & Nazzi, T. (2016). Phonetic processing when learning words: The case of bilingual infants. *International Journal of Behavioral Development, 40*, 41–52. doi:http://doi.org/10.1177/0165025415570646

Haznedar, B. (1997). L2 acquisition by a Turkish-speaking child: Evidence for L1 influence. In E. Hughes, M. Hughes, & A. Greenhill (Eds.), *Proceedings of the 21st annual Boston University conference on language development*. Somerville, MA: Cascadilla Press, 245–56.

Head Zauche, L., Darcy Mahoney, A., Thul, T., Zauche, M., Weldon, A., & Stapel-Wax, J. (2017). The power of language nutrition for children's brain development, health, and future academic achievement. *Journal of Pediatric Health Care* 31: 493–503. doi:http://doi.org/10.1016/j.pedhc.2017.01.007

Henderson, A. M. E., & Scott, J. C. (2015). She called that thing a *mido*, but should you call it a *mido* too? Linguistic experience influences infants' expectations of conventionality. *Frontiers in Psychology, 6*, 332. doi:http://doi.org/10.3389/fpsyg.2015.00332

Hoff, E., Core, C., Place, S., Rumiche, R., Señor, M., & Parra, M. (2012). Dual language exposure and early bilingual development. *Journal of Child Language, 39*, 1–27. doi:http://doi.org/10.1017/S0305000910000759

Hoff, E., Core, C., & Shanks, K. F. (2020). The quality of child-directed speech depends on the speaker's language proficiency. *Journal of Child Language, 47*, 132–145. doi:http://doi.org/10.1017/S030500091900028X

Hoff, E., & Ribot, K. M. (2017). Language growth in English monolingual and Spanish-English bilingual children from 2.5 to 5 years. *Journal of Pediatrics, 190*, 241–245.e1. doi:http://doi.org/10.1016/j.jpeds.2017.06.071

Höhle, B., Bijeljac-Babic, R., & Nazzi, T. (2020). Variability and stability in early language acquisition: Comparing monolingual and bilingual infants" speech perception and word recognition. *Bilingualism: Language and Cognition, 23*, 56–71. doi:http://doi.org/10.1017/S1366728919000348

Holowka, S., Brosseau-Lapré, F., & Petitto, L. A. (2002). Semantic and conceptual knowledge underlying bilingual babies' first signs and words. *Language Learning, 52*, 205–62. doi:http://doi.org/10.1111/0023-8333.00184

Hurtado, N., Grüter, T., Marchman, V. A., & Fernald, A. (2014). Relative language exposure, processing efficiency and vocabulary in Spanish–English bilingual toddlers. *Bilingualism: Language and Cognition, 17*(01), 189–202. doi:http://doi.org/10.1017/S136672891300014X

Idiazábal, I. (1984). Conciencia bilingüe del niño bilingüe. In M. Siguan (Ed.), *Adquisición precoz de una segunda lengua*. Barcelona: Publicacions i edicions de la universitat de Barcelona, 55–63.

Itani-Adams, Y., Iwasaki, J., & Kawaguchi, S. (2017). Similarities and differences between simultaneous and successive bilingual children: Acquisition of Japanese morphology. *International Journal of Applied Linguistics & English Literature*, *6*(7), 268–276. doi:http://doi.org/10.7575/aiac.ijalel.v.6n.7p.268

Itoh, H., & Hatch, E. (1978). Second Language Acquisition: A case study. In E. Hatch (Ed.), *Second Language Acquisition: A book of readings*. Rowley, MA: Newbury House, 77–88.

Jackson-Maldonado, D., Thal, D., Marchman, V., Bates, E., & Gutiérrez-Clellen, V. (1993). Early lexical development in Spanish-speaking infants and toddlers. *Journal of Child Language*, *20*, 523–549. doi:http://doi.org/10.1017/s0305000900008461

Jahreiß, S., Ertanir, B., Sachse, S., & Kratzmann, J. (2018). Sprachliche Interaktionen in Kindertageseinrichtungen mit hohem Anteil an mehrsprachigen Kindern. *Forschung Sprache*, 2, 32–41.

Jardak, A., & Byers-Heinlein, B. (2019). Labels or concepts? The development of semantic networks in bilingual two-year-olds. *Child Development*, *90*(2), e212–e229. doi:http://doi.org/10.1111/cdev.13050

Jia, G., Chen, J., Kim, H. Y., Chan, P.-S., & Jeung, C. (2014). Bilingual lexical skills of school-age children with Chinese and Korean heritage languages in the United States. *International Journal of Behavioral Development*, *38*, 350–358. doi:http://doi.org/10.1177/0165025414533224

Juan-Garau, M., & Lyster, R. (2019). Becoming bilingual through additive immersive programs. In A. De Houwer & L. Ortega (Eds.), *The Cambridge handbook of bilingualism*. Cambridge: Cambridge University Press, 213–232. doi:http://doi.org/10.1017/9781316831922.012

Kalashnikova, M., Escudero, P., & Kidd, E. (2018). The development of fast-mapping and novel word retention strategies in monolingual and bilingual infants. *Developmental Science*, *21*(6), e12674. doi:http://doi.org/10.1111/desc.12674

Kan, P. F., & Kohnert, K. (2005). Preschoolers learning Hmong and English: Lexical-semantic skills in L1 and L2. *Journal of Speech Language and Hearing Research*, *48*(2), 372–383. doi:http://doi.org/10.1044/1092-4388 (2005/026)

Karlsen, J., Halaas Lyster, S.-A., & Lervåg, A. (2017). Vocabulary development in Norwegian L1 and L2 learners in the kindergarten–school transition. *Journal of Child Language*, *44*(2), 402–426. doi:http://doi.org/10.1017/S0305000916000106

Karrebaek, M. S. (2013). "Don't speak like that to her!": Linguistic minority children's socialization into an ideology of monolingualism. *Journal of Sociolinguistics*, *17*(3), 355–375. doi:http://doi.org/10.1111/josl.12035

Kaufman, D. (2001). Tales of L1 attrition – Evidence from pre-puberty children. In T. Ammerlaan, M. Hulsen, H. Strating & K. Yağmur (Eds.), *Sociolinguistic and psycholinguistic perspectives on maintenance and loss of minority languages*. Münster: Waxmann, 185–202.

Kaufman, D., & Aronoff, M. (1991). Morphological disintegration and reconstruction in first language attrition. In H. Seliger & R. Vago (Eds.), *First language attrition*. Cambridge: Cambridge University Press, 175–88. doi: http://doi.org/10.1017/CBO9780511620720.012

Keller, K., Troesch, L., & Grob, A. (2013). Shyness as a risk factor for local language skills of immigrant preschoolers. *Journal of Applied Developmental Psychology*, *34*, 328–335. doi:10.1016/j.appdev.2013.07.001

Kibler, A. K., Palacios, N., & Simpson Baird, A. (2014). The influence of older siblings on language use among second generation Latino preschoolers. *TESOL Quarterly*, *48*, 164–175. doi:http://doi.org/10.1002/tesq.151

Kim, Y. K., Curby, T. W., & Winsler, A. (2014). Child, family, and school characteristics related to English proficiency development among low-income, dual language learners. *Developmental Psychology*, *50*(12), 2600–2613. doi:http://doi.org/10.1037/a0038050

Kim, Y. K., Hutchison, L. A., & Winsler, A. (2015). Bilingual education in the United States: An historical overview and examination of two-way immersion. *Educational Review*, *67*(2), 236–252. doi:http://doi.org/10.1080/00131911.2013.865593

Köppe, R. (1996). Language differentiation in bilingual children: The development of grammatical and pragmatic competence. *Linguistics*, *34*, 927–954. doi:http://doi.org/10.1515/ling.1996.34.5.927

Korecky-Kröll, K., Czinglar, C., Uzunkaya-Sharma, K., Sommer-Lolei, S., & Dressler, W. U. (2016). Das INPUT-Projekt: Wortschatz-und Grammatikerwerb von ein-und zweisprachigen Wiener Kindergartenkindern. *logoTHEMA*, *13*(1), 16–22.

Korecky-Kröll, K., Dobek, N., Blaschitz, V., Sommer-Lolei, S., Boniecki, M., Uzunkaya-Sharma, K., & Dressler, W. U. (2019). Vocabulary as a central link between phonological working memory and narrative competence: Evidence from monolingual and bilingual 4-year olds from different socioeconomic backgrounds. *Language and Speech*, *62*, 546–569. doi:http://doi.org/10.1177/0023830918796691

Kuo, E. C.-Y. (1974). The family and bilingual socialization: A sociolinguistic study of a sample of Chinese children in the United States. *The Journal of Social Psychology, 92*, 181–191.

Lanza, E. (1992). Can bilingual two-year-olds code-switch? *Journal of Child Language, 19*(3), 633–658. doi:http://doi.org/10.1017/s0305000900011600

Lauro, J., Core, C., & Hoff, E. (2020). Explaining individual differences in trajectories of simultaneous bilingual development: Contributions of child and environmental factors. *Child Development, 91*(6), 2063–2082. doi:http://doi.org/10.1111/cdev.13409

Legacy, J., Zesiger, P., Friend, M., & Poulin-Dubois, D. (2016). Vocabulary size, translation equivalents, and efficiency in word recognition in very young bilinguals. *Journal of Child Language, 43*(4), 760–783. doi:http://doi.org/10.1017/S0305000915000252

Legacy, J., Zesiger, P., Friend, M., & Poulin-Dubois, D. (2018). Vocabulary size and speed of word recognition in very young French–English bilinguals: A longitudinal study. *Bilingualism: Language and Cognition, 21*(1), 137–149. doi:http://doi.org/10.1017/S1366728916000833

Leist-Villis, A. (2004). *Zweisprachigkeit im Kontext sozialer Netzwerke. Unterstützende Rahmenbedingungen zweisprachiger Entwicklung und Erziehung am Beispiel griechisch-deutsch.* Münster: Waxmann.

Leopold, W. (1939–1949). *Speech development of a bilingual child: A linguist's record* (4 volumes). Evanston, IL: Northwestern University Press.

Levine, D., Pace, A., Luo, R., Hirsh-Pasek, K., Golinkoff, R. M., de Villiers, J., Iglesias, A., & Wilson, M. S. (2020). Evaluating socioeconomic gaps in preschoolers' vocabulary, syntax, and language process skills with the Quick Interactive Language Screener (QUILS). *Early Childhood Research Quarterly, 50*, 114–128. doi:http://doi.org/10.1016/j.ecresq.2018.11.006

Liberman, Z., Woodward, A. L., Keysar, B., & Kinzler, K. D. (2017). Exposure to multiple languages enhances communication skills in infancy. *Developmental Science, 20*, e12420. doi:http://doi.org/10.1111/desc.12420

Linberg, T., Schneider, T., Waldfogel, J., & Wang, Y. (2019). Socioeconomic status gaps in child cognitive development in Germany and the United States. *Social Science Research, 79*, 1–31. doi:http://doi.org/10.1016/j.ssresearch.2018.11.002

Lindquist, H., & Gram Garmann, N. (2021). Toddlers and their translingual practicing homes. *International Journal of Multilingualism, 18*(1), 59–72. doi:http://doi.org/10.1080/14790718.2019.1604712

Liu, L., & Kager, R. (2017). Perception of tones by bilingual infants learning non-tone languages. *Bilingualism: Language and Cognition, 20*, 561–575. doi:http://doi.org/10.1017/S1366728916000183

Li Wei. (2011). The early acquisition of English as a second language: The case of young Chinese learners of English in Britain. In A. De Houwer & A. Wilton (Eds.), *English in Europe today: Educational and sociocultural perspectives*. Amsterdam: John Benjamins, 105–122. doi:http://doi.org/10.1075/aals.8.07wei

Luo, R., Escobar, K., & Tamis-LeMonda, C. S. (2020). Heterogeneity in the trajectories of US Latine mothers" dual-language input from infancy to preschool. *First Language*, *40*(3), 275–99. doi:http://doi.org/10.1177/0142723720915401

MacLeod,A. A. N., Fabiano-Smith, L., Boegner-Pagé, S., & Fontolliet, S. (2013). Simultaneous bilingual language acquisition: The role of parental input on receptive vocabulary development. *Child Language Teaching and Therapy*, *29*, 131–142. doi:http://doi.org/10.1177/0265659012466862

MacSwan, J., & Pray, L. (2005). Learning English bilingually: Age of onset of exposure and rate of acquisition among English language learners in a bilingual education program. *Bilingual Research Journal*, *29*(3), 653–678. doi:http://doi.org/10.1080/15235882.2005.10162857

Mancilla-Martinez, J., & Lesaux, N. (2011). The gap between Spanish speakers" word reading and word knowledge: A longitudinal study. *Child Development*, *82*(5),1544–1560. doi:http://doi.org/10.1111/j.1467-8624.2011.01633.x

Maneva, B., & Genesee, F. (2002). Bilingual babbling: Evidence for language differentiation in dual language acquisition. In B. Skarbela, S. Fish, & A H.-J Do (Eds.), *Boston University Conference on Language Development 26 Proceedings*. Sommerville, MA: Cascadilla Press, 383–392.

Manigand, A. (1999). Le silence des enfants turcs à l'école. *Psychologie & Éducation*, *37*, 57–73.

Marchman, V. A., Bermúdez, V. N., Bang, J. Y., & Fernald, A. (2020). Off to a good start: Early Spanish-language processing efficiency supports Spanish- and English-language outcomes at 4½ years in sequential bilinguals. *Developmental Science*, *23*(6) e12973. doi:http://doi.org/10.1111/desc.12973

Marchman, V. A., Fernald, A., & Hurtado, N. (2010). How vocabulary size in two languages relates to efficiency in spoken word recognition by young Spanish–English bilinguals. *Journal of Child Language*, *37*(04), 817–840. doi:http://doi.org/10.1017/S0305000909990055

Marchman, V., Martínez, L., Hurtado, N., Grüter, T., & Fernald, A. (2017). Caregiver talk to young Spanish-English bilinguals: Comparing direct observation and parent-report measures of dual-language exposure. *Developmental Science*, *20*(1), e12425. doi:http://doi.org/10.1111/desc.12425

Marchman, V. A., Martínez-Sussmann, C., & Dale, P. S. (2004). The language-specific nature of grammatical development: Evidence from bilingual language learners. *Developmental Science*, *7*, 212–224. doi:http://doi.org/10.1111/j.1467-7687.2004.00340.x

Marecka, M., Wrembel, M., Otwinowska, A., Szewczyk, J., Banasik-Jemielniak, N., & Wodniecka, Z. (2020). Bilingual children's phonology shows evidence of transfer, but not deceleration in their L1. *Studies in Second Language Acquisition*, *42*(1), 89–114. doi:http://doi.org/10.1017/S0272263119000408

Markman, E. M., & Wachtel, G. F. (1988). Children's use of mutual exclusivity to constrain the meanings of words. *Cognitive Psychology*, *20*, 121–157. doi:http://doi.org/10.1016/0010-0285(88)90017-5

Marinis, T., Armon-Lotem,S., & Pontikas, G. (Eds.) (2017). Language impairment in bilingual children: State of the art 2017. Special Issue. *Linguistic Approaches to Bilingualism*, *7* (3–4). doi:http://doi.org/10.1075/lab.7.3-4

Mayr, R., & Montanari, S. (2015). Cross-linguistic interaction in trilingual phonological development: The role of the input in the acquisition of the voicing contrast. *Journal of Child Language*, *42*(5), 1006–1035. doi:http://doi.org/10.1017/S0305000914000592

Meisel, J. M. (1989). Early differentiation of languages in bilingual children. In K. Hyltenstam & L. K. Obler (Eds.), *Bilingualism across the lifespan: Aspects of acquisition, maturity and loss*. Cambridge: Cambridge University Press, 13–40. doi:http://doi.org/10.1017/CBO9780511611780.003

Meisel, J. M. (2008). Âge du début de l'acquisition successive du bilinguisme. Effets sur le développement grammatical. In M. Kail, M. Fayol, & M. Hickman (Eds.), *Apprentissage des langues premières et secondes*. Paris: Editions du CNRS, 245–272.

Meisel, J. M., Elsig, M., & Bonnesen, M. (2011). Delayed grammatical acquisition in first language development: Subject-verb inversion and subject clitics in French interrogatives. *Linguistic Approaches to Bilingualism*, *1*(4), 347–390. doi:http://doi.org/10.1075/lab.1.4.01mei

Mirvahedi, S. H., & Cavallaro, F. (2020). Siblings' play and language shift to English in a Malay-English bilingual family. *World Englishes*, *39*(1), 183–197. doi:http://doi.org/10.1111/weng.12417

Mishina, S. (1999). The role of parental input and discourse strategies in the early language mixing of a bilingual child. *Multilingua*, *18*(4), 343–367. doi:http://doi.org/10.1515/mult.1999.18.4.317

Mobaraki, M., Vainikka, A., & Young-Scholten, M. (2008). The status of subjects in early child L2 English. In B. Haznedar & E. Gavruseva (Eds.), *Current trends in child second language acquisition: A generative perspective*. Amsterdam: John Benjamins, 209–236. doi:http://doi.org/10 .1075/lald.46.11mob

Montanari, S. (2010). Translation equivalents and the emergence of multiple lexicons in early trilingual development. *First Language*, *30*, 102–125. doi: http://doi.org/10.1177/0142723709350528

Müller, L.-M., Howard, K., Wilson, E., Gibson, J., & Katsos, N. (2020). Bilingualism in the family and child well-being: A scoping review. *International Journal of Bilingualism*, *24*(5–6), 1049–1070. doi:http://doi .org/10.1177/1367006920920939

Muñoz, C., & Spada, N. (2019). Foreign language learning from early child-hood to young adulthood. In A. De Houwer & L. Ortega (Eds.), *The Cambridge handbook of bilingualism*. Cambridge: Cambridge University Press, 233–249. doi:http://doi.org/10.1017/9781316831922.013

Murphy, V. A. (2018). Literacy development in linguistically diverse pupils. In D. Miller, F. Bayram, J. Rothman, & L. Serratrice (Eds.), *Bilingual cognition and language: The state of the science across its subfields*. Amsterdam: John Benjamins, 155–82. doi:http://doi.org/10.1075/sibil .54.08mur

Nakamura, J. (2015). Nonnative maternal input : Language use and errors in a Thai mother's interactions in Japanese with her child. *Japan Journal of Multilingualism and Multiculturalism*, *21*, 10–26.

Nakamura, J. (2020). Language regrets: Mixed-ethnic children's lost opportun-ity for minority language acquisition in Japan. *Multilingua*, *39*(2), 213–237. doi:http://doi.org/10.1515/multi-2019-0040

Nakamura, J., & Quay, S. (2012). The impact of caregivers' interrogative styles in English and Japanese on early bilingual development. *International Journal of Bilingual Education and Bilingualism*, *15*(4), 417–434. doi: http://doi.org/10.1080/13670050.2012.665827

Navarro, A. M., Pearson, B. Z., Cobo-Lewis, A., & Oller, K. D. (1998). Identifying the language spoken by 26-month-old monolingual- and bilin-gual-learning babies in a no-context situation. In A. Greenhill, M. Hughes, H. Littlefield, & H. Walsh (Eds.), *Proceedings of the 22nd Annual Boston University Conference on Language Development*, Vol. 2. Somerville, MA: Cascadilla Press, 557–68.

Nicoladis, E. (1998). First clues to the existence of two input languages: Pragmatic and lexical differentiation in a bilingual child. *Bilingualism: Language and Cognition*, *1*(2), 105–116. doi:http://doi.org/10.1017 /S1366728998000236

Oller, D. K., & Eilers, R. E. (Eds.) (2002). *Language and literacy in bilingual children*. Clevedon: Multilingual Matters.

Oppenheim, G. M., Griffin, Z. M., Peña, E. D., & Bedore, L. M. (2020). Longitudinal evidence for simultaneous bilingual language development with shifting language dominance, and how to explain it. *Language Learning, 70,* 20–44. doi:http://doi.org/10.1111/lang.12398

Orena, A., Byers-Heinlein, K., & Polka, L. (2020). What do bilingual infants actually hear? Evaluating measures of language input to bilingual-learning 10-month-olds. *Developmental Science 23*(2), e12901. doi:http://doi.org/10.31234/osf.io/2qnhw

Orena, A. J., & Polka, L. (2019). Monolingual and bilingual infants" word segmentation abilities in an inter-mixed dual-language task. *Infancy, 24*(5), 718–737. doi:http://doi.org/10.1111/infa.12296

Pace, A., Luo, R., Hirsh-Pasek, K., & Golinkoff, R.M. (2017). Identifying pathways between socio-economic status and language development. *Annual Review of Linguistics, 3,* 285–308. doi:http://doi.org/10.1146/annurev-linguistics-011516-034226

Palacios, N., Kibler, A. K., Simpson Baird, A., Parr, A., & Bergey, R. (2015). An examination of language practices during mother-child play activities among Mexican immigrant families. *International Multilingual Research Journal, 9*(3), 197–219. doi:http://doi.org/10.1080/19313152.2015.1048543

Paradis, J. (2011). Individual differences in child English second language acquisition: Comparing child-internal and child-external factors. *Linguistic Approaches to Bilingualism, 1*(3), 213–237. doi:http://doi.org/10.1075/lab.1.3.01par

Paradis, J., & Navarro, S. (2003). Subject realization and crosslinguistic interference in the bilingual acquisition of Spanish and English: What is the role of the input? *Journal of Child Language, 30,* 371–393. doi:http://doi.org/10.1017/S0305000903005609

Paradis, J., & Nicoladis, E. (2007). The influence of dominance and sociolinguistic context on bilingual preschoolers" language choice. *The International Journal of Bilingual Education and Bilingualism, 10*(3), 277–297. doi:http://doi.org/10.2167/beb444.0

Park, H., Tsai, K. M., Liu, L. L., & Lau, A. S. (2012). Transactional associations between supportive family climate and young children's heritage language proficiency in immigrant families. *International Journal of Behavioral Development, 36*(3), 226–236. doi:http://doi.org/10.1177/0165025412439842

Parra, M., Hoff, E., & Core, C. (2011). Relations among language exposure, phonological memory, and language development in Spanish-English bilingually developing two year olds. *Journal of Experimental Child Psychology, 108,* 113–125. doi:http://doi.org/10.1016/j.jecp.2010.07.011

Patterson, J. L. (1998). Expressive vocabulary development and word combinations of Spanish–English bilingual toddlers. *American Journal of Speech–Language Pathology*, *7*, 46–56. doi:http://doi.org/10.1044/1058-0360.0704.46

Patterson, J. L. (2002). Relationships of expressive vocabulary to frequency of reading and television experience among bilingual toddlers. *Applied Psycholinguistics*, *23*(4), 493–508. doi:http://doi.org/10.1017/S0142716402004010

Patterson, J. L, & Rodríguez, B. L. (Eds.) (2016). *Multilingual perspectives on child language disorders*. Bristol: Multilingual Matters. doi:http://doi.org/10.21832/9781783094738

Pavlovitch, M. (1920). *Le langage enfantin. Acquisition du serbe et du français*. Paris: Champion.

Pearson, B. Z., & Fernández, S. C. (1994). Patterns of interaction in the lexical growth in two languages of bilingual infants and toddlers. *Language Learning*, *44*, 617–653.

Pearson, B. Z., Fernández, S., Lewedeg, V., & Oller, D. K. (1997). The relation of input factors to lexical learning by bilingual infants. *Applied Psycholinguistics*, *18*, 41–58. doi:http://doi.org/10.1017/S0142716400009863

Pearson, B. Z., Fernández, S., & Oller, D. K. (1993). Lexical development in simultaneous bilingual infants: comparison to monolinguals. *Language Learning*, *43*, 93–120.

Pearson, B. Z., Fernández, S., & Oller, D. K. (1995). Cross-language synonyms in the lexicons of bilingual infants: One language or two? *Journal of Child Language*, *22*, 345–368. doi:http://doi.org/10.1017/S030500090000982X

Pearson, P. D. (2019). Time, complexity, and the enduring importance of words: Key themes in language learning in the middle years. In V. Grøver, P. Ucelli, M. L. Rowe, & E. Lieven (Eds.), *Learning through language. Towards an educationally informed theory of language learning*. Cambridge: Cambridge University Press, 159–169. doi:http://doi.org/10.1017/9781316718537.015

Pease-Alvarez, L., & Winsler, A. (1994). Cuando el maestro no habla Español: Children's bilingual languages practices in the classroom. *TESOL Quarterly*, *28*, 507–535.

Persici, V., Vihman, M. M., Burroa, R., & Majoranoa, M. (2019). Lexical access and competition in bilingual children: The role of proficiency and the lexical similarity of the two languages. *Journal of Experimental Child Psychology*, *179*, 103–125. doi:http://doi.org/10.1016/j.jecp.2018.10.002

Pfaff, C. (1994). Early bilingual development of Turkish children in Berlin. In G. Extra & L. Verhoeven (Eds.), *The cross-linguistic study of bilingualism*. Amsterdam: Royal Netherlands Academy of Arts and Sciences, 75–97.

Pienemann, M. (1981). *Der Zweitspracherwerb ausländischer Arbeiterkinder.* Bonn: Bouvier.

Place, S., & Hoff, E. (2011). Properties of dual language exposure that influence two-year-olds' bilingual proficiency. *Child Development, 82 (6)*, 1834–1849. doi:http://doi.org/10.1111/j.1467-8624.2011.01660.x

Place, S., & Hoff, E. (2016). Effects and noneffects of input in bilingual environments on dual language skills in 2½-year-olds. *Bilingualism: Language and Cognition*, 19, 1023–1041. doi:http://doi.org/10.1017/s1366728915000322

Polka, L., Orena, A. J., Sundara, M., & Worrall, J. (2017). Segmenting words from fluent speech during infancy – challenges and opportunities in a bilingual context. *Developmental Science*, 20, e12419. doi:http://doi.org/10.1111/desc.12419

Porsché, D. (1983). *Die Zweisprachigkeit während des primären Spracherwerbs.* Tübingen: Gunter Narr.

Prevoo, M. J. L., Malda, M., Mesman, J., Emmen, R.A.G., Yeniad, N., van IJzendoorn, M. H., & Linting, M. (2014). Predicting ethnic minority children's vocabulary from socioeconomic status, maternal language and home reading input: Different pathways for host and ethnic language. *Journal of Child Language*, 41(5), 963–984. doi:http://doi.org/10.1017/S0305000913000299

Prevoo, M., Mesman, J., van IJzendoorn,M., & Pieper, S. (2011). Bilingual toddlers reap the language they sow: Ethnic minority toddlers' childcare attendance increases maternal host language use. *Journal of Multilingual and Multicultural Development*, 32, 561–576. doi:http://doi.org/10.1080/01434632.2011.609279

Poulin-Dubois, D., Bialystok, E., Blaye, A., Polonia, A., & Yott, J. (2013). Lexical access and vocabulary development in very young bilinguals. *International Journal of Bilingualism, 17*(1), 57–70. doi:http://doi.org/10.1177/1367006911431198

Ramírez-Esparza, N., García-Sierra, A., & Kuhl, P. K. (2017). The impact of early social interactions on later language development in Spanish–English bilingual infants. *Child Development, 88*(4), 1216–1234. doi:http://doi.org/10.1111/cdev.12648

Reich, H. H. (2009). *Zweisprachige Kinder. Sprachenaneignung und sprachliche Fortschritte im Kindergartenalter.* Münster: Waxmann.

Ribot, K., & Hoff, E. (2014). "¿Cómo estas?" "I'm good." Conversational code-switching is related to profiles of expressive and receptive proficiency in Spanish-English bilingual toddlers. *International Journal of Behavioral Development, 38*(3), 333–341. doi:http://doi.org/10.1177/0165025414533225

Ribot, K. M., Hoff, E., & Burridge, A. (2018). Language use contributes to expressive language growth: evidence from bilingual children. *Child Development, 89*(3), 929–940. doi:http://doi.org/10.1111/cdev.12770

Rinker, T., Budde-Spengler, N., & Sachse, S. (2017). The relationship between first language (L1) and second language (L2) lexical development in young Turkish-German children. *International Journal of Bilingualism and Bilingual Education, 20*, 218–233. doi:http://doi.org/10.1080/13670050 .2016.1179260

Roesch, A., & Condrogianni, V. (2016). "Which mouse kissed the frog?" Effects of age of onset, length of exposure, and knowledge of case marking on the comprehension of wh-questions in German-speaking simultaneous and early sequential bilingual children. *Journal of Child Language, 43*(3), 635–661. doi:http://doi.org/10.1017/S0305000916000015

Ronjat, J. (1913). *Le développement du langage observé chez un enfant bilingue*. Paris: Champion.

Rothweiler, M. (2016). Zum Erwerb der deutschen Grammatik bei früh sequentiell zweisprachigen Kindern mit Türkisch als Erstsprache – Ergebnisse aus einem Forschungsprojekt. *Diskurs Kindheits- und Jugendforschung, 1*, 9-25.

Scheele, A., Leseman, P., & Mayo, A. (2010). The home language environment of monolingual and bilingual children and their language proficiency. *Applied Psycholinguistics, 31*, 117–140. doi:http://doi.org/10.1017 /S0142716409990191

Schulz, P. (2013). Wer versteht wann was? Sprachverstehen im frühen Zweitspracherwerb des Deutschen am Beispiel der w-Fragen. In A. Deppermann (Ed.), *Das Deutsch der Migranten*. Berlin: de Gruyter, 313–337. doi:http://doi.org/10.1515/9783110307894.313

Schulz, P., & Tracy, R. (2011). *LiSe-DaZ. Linguistische Sprachstandserhebung – Deutsch als Zweitsprache. (In Verbindung mit der Baden-Württemberg Stiftung)*. Göttingen: Hogrefe.

Schwartz, M. (2020). Strategies and practices of home language maintenance. In S. Eisenchlas & A. Schalley (Eds.), *Handbook of home language maintenance and development. Social and affective factors*. Berlin: Mouton de Gruyter, 194–217. doi:http://doi.org/10.1515/9781501510175-010

Schwartz, M., Deeb, I., & Hijazy, S. (2020). "How do you say it in Arabic, in Hebrew, in English?" Towards a better understanding of children's agentic behaviour in novel language learning. *Journal of Multilingual and Multicultural Development*. doi:http://doi.org/10.1080/01434632.2020.1711768

Schwartz, M., Minkov, M., Dieser, E., Protassova, E., Moin, V., & Polinsky, M. (2015). Acquisition of Russian gender agreement by monolingual and bilingual children. *International Journal of Bilingualism, 19*, 726–752. doi: http://doi.org/10.1177/1367006914544989

Serratrice, L. (2007). Cross-linguistic influence in the interpretation of anaphoric and cataphoric pronouns in English–Italian bilingual children. *Bilingualism: Language and Cognition, 10*, 225–238. doi:http://doi.org/10.1017/S1366728907003045

Serratrice, L. (2019). Becoming bilingual in early childhood. In A. De Houwer & L. Ortega (Eds.), *The Cambridge handbook of bilingualism*. Cambridge: Cambridge University Press, 15–35. doi:http://doi.org/10.1017/9781316831922.002

Sierens, S., Slembrouck, S., Van Gorp, K., & Ağırdağ, O. (2019). Linguistic interdependence of receptive vocabulary skills in emergent bilingual preschool children: Exploring a factor-dependent approach. *Applied Psycholinguistics, 50*(5), 1269–1297. doi:http://doi.org/10.1017/S0142716419000250

Silvén, M., Voeten, M., Kouvo, A., & Lundén, M. (2014). Speech perception and vocabulary growth: A longitudinal study of Finnish-Russian bilinguals and Finnish monolinguals from infancy to three years. *International Journal of Behavioral Development, 38*(4), 323–332. doi:http://doi.org/10.1177/0165025414533748

Singh, L., Fu, C.S.L., Tay, Z., & Golinkoff, R. M. (2017). Novel word learning in bilingual and monolingual infants: Evidence for a bilingual advantage. *Child Development, 89*(3), e183–e198. doi:http://doi.org/10.1111/cdev.12747

Singh, L., Poh, F. L. S., & Fu, C. S. L. (2016). Limits on monolingualism? A comparison of monolingual and bilingual infants' abilities to integrate lexical tone in novel word learning. *Frontiers in Psychology, 7*, 667. doi: http://doi.org/10.3389/fpsyg.2016.00667

Sinka, I., & Schelletter, C. (1998). Morphosyntactic development in bilingual children. *International Journal of Bilingualism, 2*(3), 301–326. doi:http://doi.org/10.1177/136700699800200303

Slavkov, N. (2015). Language attrition and reactivation in the context of bilingual first language acquisition. *International Journal of Bilingual Education and Bilingualism, 18*, 715–734. doi:http://doi.org/10.1080/13670050.2014.941785

Smithson, L., Paradis, J., & Nicoladis, E. (2014). Bilingualism and receptive vocabulary achievement: Could sociocultural context make a difference? *Bilingualism: Language and Cognition, 17*(4), 810–821. doi:http://doi.org/10.1017/S1366728913000813

Song, L., Tamis-LeMonda, C. S., Yoshikawa, H., Kahana-Kalman, R., & Wu, I. (2012). Language experiences and vocabulary development in Dominican and Mexican infants across the first 2 years. *Developmental Psychology, 48,* 1106–1123. doi:http://doi.org/10.1037/a0026401

Steinberg, L., Bornstein, M. H., Vandell, D. L., & Rook, K. (2011). *Life-span development: Infancy through adulthood.* Boston, MA: Wadsworth Cengage Learning.

Sun, H., Ng, S. C., O'Brien, B. A., & Fritzsche, T. (2020). Child, family, and school factors in bilingual preschoolers' vocabulary development in heritage languages. *Journal of Child Language, 47*(4), 817–843. doi:http://doi.org/10.1017/S0305000919000904

Sun, H., Yussof, N., Mohamed, M., Rahim, A., Cheung, W. L., Cheong, S. A., & Bull, R. (2021). Bilingual language experience and social-emotional well-being: A cross-sectional study of Singapore preschoolers. *International Journal of Bilingual Education and Bilingualism, 24*(3), 324–339. doi: http://doi.org/10.1080/13670050.2018.1461802

Sundara, M., Polka, L., & Genesee, F. (2006). Language-experience facilitates discrimination of /d-δ/ in monolingual and bilingual acquisition of English. *Cognition, 100*(2), 369–388. doi:http://doi.org/10.1016/j.cognition.2005.04.007

Sundara, M., & Scutellaro, A. (2011). Rhythmic distance between languages affects the development of speech perception in bilingual infants. *Journal of Phonetics, 39*(4), 505–513. doi:http://doi.org/10.1016/j.wocn.2010.08.006

Sundara, M., Ward, N., Conboy, B., & Kuhl, P. K. (2020). Exposure to a second language in infancy alters speech production. *Bilingualism: Language and Cognition, 23*(5), 978–991. doi:http://doi.org/10.1017/S1366728919000853

Tang, G., & Sze, F. (2019). Bilingualism and sign language research. In A. De Houwer & L. Ortega (Eds.), *The Cambridge handbook of bilingualism.* Cambridge: Cambridge University Press, 483–509. doi:http://doi.org/10.1017/9781316831922.025

Tare, M., & Gelman, S. A. (2010). Can you say it another way? Cognitive factors in bilingual children's pragmatic language skills. *Journal of Cognition and Development, 11,* 137–158.

Thompson, L. (2000). *Young bilingual children in nursery school.* Clevedon: Multilingual Matters.

Uccelli, P., & Páez, M. (2007). Narrative and vocabulary development of bilingual children from kindergarten to first grade: Developmental changes and associations among English and Spanish skills. *Language, Speech, and Hearing Services in Schools, 38,* 225–236. doi:http://doi.org/10.1044/0161-1461(2007/024)

Uchikoshi, Y. (2006). English vocabulary development in bilingual kindergarteners: What are the best predictors? *Bilingualism: Language and Cognition, 9,* 33–49. doi:http://doi.org/10.1017/S1366728905002361

UNESCO. (2016). *If you don't understand, how can you learn?* Global Education Monitoring Report. Policy Paper 24. bit.ly/MLD2016

Unsworth, S. (2013). Assessing age of onset effects in (early) child L2 acquisition. *Language Acquisition, 20,* 74–92. doi:http://doi.org/10.1080/10489223.2013.766739

Unsworth, S., Argyri, F., Cornips, L., Hulk, A., Sorace, A., & Tsimpli, I. (2014). The role of age of onset and input in early child bilingualism in Greek and Dutch. *Applied Psycholinguistics, 35,* 765–805. doi:http://doi.org/10.1017/S0142716412000574

Unsworth, S., Brouwer, S., de Bree, E. & Verhagen, J. (2019). Predicting bilingual preschoolers' patterns of language development: Degree of non-native input matters. *Applied Psycholinguistics, 40*(5), 1189–1219. doi:http://doi.org/10.1017/S0142716419000225

Vaahtoranta, E., Suggate, S., Lenhart, J., & Lenhard, W. (2020). Language exposure and phonological short-term memory as predictors of majority language vocabulary and phonological awareness in dual language learning. *Bilingualism: Language and Cognition, 24*(2), 319–332. doi:http://doi.org/10.1017/S1366728920000541

van de Weijer, J. (1997). Language input to a prelingual infant. In A. Sorace, C. Heycock & R. Shillcock (Eds.), *Proceedings of the GALA '97 Conference on Language Acquisition.* Edinburgh: University of Edinburgh, 290–293.

van de Weijer, J. (1998). *Language input for word discovery.* Max Planck Series in Psycholinguistics 9. Wageningen: Ponsen & Looijen.

van de Weijer, J. (2000). Language input and word discovery. In M. Beers, B. van den Bogaerde, G. Bol, J. de Jong, & C. Rooijmans (Eds.), *From sound to sentence: Studies on first language acquisition.* Groningen: Centre for Language and Cognition, 155–162.

van de Weijer, J. (2002). How much does an infant hear in a day? In J. Costa & M. João Freitas (Eds.), *Proceedings of the GALA2001 Conference on Language Acquisition.* Lisbon, Portugal: Associação Portuguesa de Linguistíca, 279–282.

Verdon, S., McLeod, S., & Winsler, A. (2014). Language maintenance and loss in a population study of young Australian children. *Early Childhood Research Quarterly, 29*(2), 168–181. doi:http://doi.org/10.1016/j.ecresq.2013.12.003

Vihman, M. M. (1999). The transition to grammar in a bilingual child: Positional patterns, model learning, and relational words. *International Journal of Bilingualism, 3*(2–3), 267–301. doi:http://doi.org/10.1177/13670069990030020801

Vihman, M. (2016). Prosodic structures and templates in bilingual phonological development. *Bilingualism: Language and Cognition, 19*, 69–88. doi:http://doi.org/10.1017/S1366728914000790

Vihman, M. M., Thierry, G., Lum, J., Keren-Portnoy, T., & Martin, P. (2007). Onset of word form recognition in English, Welsh, and English-Welsh bilingual infants. *Applied Psycholinguistics, 28*, 475–493. doi:http://doi.org/10.1017/S0142716407070269

Vila, I. (1984). Yo siempre hablo catalan y castellano: datos de una investigacion en curso sobre la adquisicion del lenguaje en niños bilingües familiares. In M. Siguan (Ed.), *Adquisición precoz de una segunda lengua*. Barcelona: Publicacions i edicions de la Universitat de Barcelona, 31–51.

von Grünigen, R., Kochenderfer-Ladd, B., Perren, S., & Alsaker, F. (2012). Links between local language competence and peer relations among Swiss and immigrant children: The mediating role of social behaviour. *Journal of School Psychology, 50*(2), 195–213. doi:http://doi.org/10.1016/j.jsp.2011.09.005

Wagner-Gough, J. (1975). *Comparative studies in second language learning*. CAL-ERIC/CCL Series on Language and Linguistics, 26. Washington, DC: Center for Applied Linguistics.

Weikum, W. M., Vouloumanos, A., Navarra, J., Soto-Faraco, S., Sebastián-Gallés, N., & Werker, J. F. (2007). Visual language discrimination in infancy. *Science, 316*(5828), 1159. doi:http://doi.org/10.1126/science.1137686

Willard, J. A., Kohl, K., Bihler, L.-M., Agache, A., & Leyendecker, B. (2020). Family literacy activities and their interplay with family and preschool language environments: Links to gains in dual language learners' German vocabulary. *Early Education and Development, 32*(2), 189–208. doi:http://doi.org/10.1080/10409289.2020.1744404

Winsler, A., Burchinal, M., Tien, H.-C., Peisner-Feinberg, E., Espinosa, L., Castro, D., LaForett, D., Kim, Y., & De Feyter, J. (2014a). Early developmental skills of diverse dual language learners: The roles of home language use, cultural heritage, maternal immigration, and socio-demographic variables. *Early Childhood Research Quarterly, 29*, 750–764. doi:http://dx.doi.org/10.1016/j.ecresq.2014.02.008

Winsler, A., Kim, Y., & Richard, E. (2014b). Socio-emotional skills, behavior problems, and Spanish competence predict the acquisition of English among English language learners in poverty. *Developmental Psychology, 50*, 2242–2254. doi:http://doi.org/10.1037/a0037161

Wölck, W. (1987/1988). Types of natural bilingual behavior: A review and revision. *The Bilingual Review/La Revista bilingüe, 14*, 3–16.

Yamamoto, M. (2001). *Language use in interlingual families: A Japanese–English sociolinguistic study.* Clevedon: Multilingual Matters.

Yow, W. Q., & Markman, E. M. (2011). Young bilingual children's heightened sensitivity to referential cues. *Journal of Cognitive Development*, *12*, 12–31. doi:http://doi.org/10.1080/15248372.2011.539524

Yu, S. (2014). How much can migrant parents influence their children's language choice. *Taiwan Journal of Linguistics*, *12*(1), 81–105.

Zdorenko, T., & Paradis, J. (2007). The role of the first language in child second language acquisition of articles. In A. Belikova, L. Meroni, & M. Umeda (Eds.), *Galana 2: Proceedings of the Conference on Generative Approaches to Language Acquisition North America 2.* Somerville, MA: Cascadilla Proceedings Project, 483-490.

Zentella, A. C. (1997). *Growing up bilingual: Puerto Rican children in New York.* Oxford: Wiley-Blackwell.

Cambridge Elements ☰

Child Development

Marc H. Bornstein

National Institute of Child Health and Human Development, Bethesda
Institute for Fiscal Studies, London
UNICEF, New York City

Marc H. Bornstein is an Affiliate of the Eunice Kennedy Shriver National Institute of Child Health and Human Development, an International Research Fellow at the Institute for Fiscal Studies (London), and UNICEF Senior Advisor for Research for ECD Parenting Programmes. Bornstein is President Emeritus of the Society for Research in Child Development, Editor Emeritus of *Child Development*, and founding Editor of *Parenting: Science and Practice.*

About the Series

Child development is a lively and engaging, yet serious and purposeful subject of academic study that encompasses a myriad of theories, methods, substantive areas, and applied concerns. Cambridge Elements in Child Development proposes to address all these key areas, with unique, comprehensive, and state-of-the-art treatments, introducing readers to the primary currents of research and to original perspectives on, or contributions to, principal issues and domains in the field

Cambridge Elements ≡

Child Development

Printed in the United States
by Baker & Taylor Publisher Services